Outside

First edition 2014
Text copyright © Maria Ana Peixe Dias and Inês Teixeira do Rosário
Illustrations copyright © Bernardo P. Carvalho

The right of Maria Ana Peixe Dias, Inês Teixeira do Rosário, and Bernardo P. Carvalho to be identified as the authors and illustrator of this work has been asserted by them in accordance with the Copyright, Designs and Patents Act, 1988 (United Kingdom).

Published with the permission of Planeta Tangerina
Rua das Rosas, n.° 20, Alto dos Lombos, 2775-683 Carcavelos, Portugal

Funded by the Dirção-Geral do Livro, dos Arquivos e das Bibliotecas/Portugal

GOVERNO DE **PORTUGAL** | SECRETÁRIO DE E DA CULTURA

DIREÇÃO-GERAL DO LIVRO, DOS ARQUI\
DAS BIBLIOTECAS

This paperback edition first published in Great Britain in 2018 by Lincoln Children's Books,
6 Blundell Street N79BH
QuartoKnows.com
Visit our blogs at QuartoKnows.com

A catalogue record for this book is available from the British Library.

ISBN 978-1-78603-160-0

Designed by Planeta Tangerina
Translated by Lucy Greaves
Original edition edited by Isabel Minhós Martins and Carlos Grifo Babo
English language edition edited by Jenny Broom

Natural history consultancy:
Ana Francisco, Sérgio Chozas and Paulo Cardoso – SPBotânica ("Flowers")
Maria João Pereira ("Mammals")
Mário Boieiro (animals and "Bugs and Critters")
Miguel Lecoq, Paulo Catry, Ricardo Tomé ("Birds")
Nuno Pedroso ("Follow The Clues" and "Mammals")
Ricardo Calado ("Beaches, Oceans, and Tidepools")
Rui Rebelo ("Amphibeans" and "Reptiles")
Sónia Anton ("The Stars, the Moon and the Sun")
Teresa Leal Rosa ("Clouds, Wind and Rain")
Teresa Melo ("Rocks")

Printed in China

9 8 7 6 5 4 3 2 1

FSC | MIX
Paper from responsible sources
FSC® C101537

OUTSIDE

DISCOVERING ANIMALS

Maria Ana Peixe Dias

Inês Teixeira Do Rosário

Bernardo P. Carvalho

Translated by Lucy Greaves

Lincoln
Children's Books

Animals . . . where are you?

Even if we live in the middle of the biggest city in the world, surrounded by big roads full of cars, there's always nature outside. The sky and stars (even if they're hidden by skyscrapers), clouds and rain, trees and flowers, and animals, lots of animals, are always there.

Animals? Where are they? (I never see them when I go out!)

Much of the time we're so distracted or in such a hurry that we don't even notice the small birds flying noisily above us, or the bats fluttering around a streetlight at dusk.

There are animals everywhere, but of course there are places where there are more of them and where they are easier to find. If you live in the country, you know this very well. All you have to do is walk away from the houses a little bit and you'll start to see different animals and plants.

In a city, there aren't so many different species, but they are still there . . . You just have to know where to look and, above all, you have to pay attention.

Yards and gardens are the easiest places to start, and most times you will find birds, small mammals, lizards, hundreds of insects, and other critters—on the ground, in the trees, or on plants.

If you want to see more species, or see a sky that will take your breath away, the best thing to do is go to the country: wherever you live, you can get to a forest, a river, or a mountain without traveling too far.

There's no limit to what we can learn outside. That might seem like an exaggeration, but it isn't. Every time we answer a question, many more arise. That's why the number of questions we can ask is infinite. In this book, we don't want to (and we wouldn't be able to!) answer all of them. We'll answer some, but many more will occur when you go outside.

Any plant you find, any tree you climb, any small creature you see has a story to tell and will make you ask lots of questions.

You might say, "But animals don't talk!" Maybe not, at least not in a language we're able to understand right away, but this only makes the challenge more interesting.

Just like what happens when we hear a foreign language for the first time, we should also listen carefully to the language of nature. If we keep our senses alert, we'll be able to tell what plants, animals, stars, rocks, and everything else around us is saying.

In putting together this book, we paid particular attention to living things. That's our favorite topic and also the one that grabs the most attention when we go outside: the animals that pass by, the clues they leave, the trees that shelter them, and so on.

Why did we decide to write this book?

It might seem that nothing is happening outside and that everything happens indoors: inside, we've got books, TV, computers, video games, movies . . .

But maybe that's not actually the case!

If you pay a little more attention—and this might be a different kind of attention than the one you use when you're watching TV or playing a computer game—you'll notice that *everything* is happening outside: the earth is spinning, clouds are moving, plants are sprouting up and dying, animals are busy going through their routines . . . We just have to make a little effort to learn to watch, and in the end, it can be much more rewarding than spending an afternoon on the sofa. (Of course, a screen can open up a whole world, but let's be clear: life on a screen is not the same as life in an anthill or a rock pool.)

We want this book to work as an incentive to leave the house. And we don't want it to become just a pretty display where you can see pictures of birds, clouds, or flowers. We want it to be a guide with ideas and practical information that will help you explore what you find outside.

**There's a whole world of animals waiting for you out there.
We hope you have lots of adventures!**

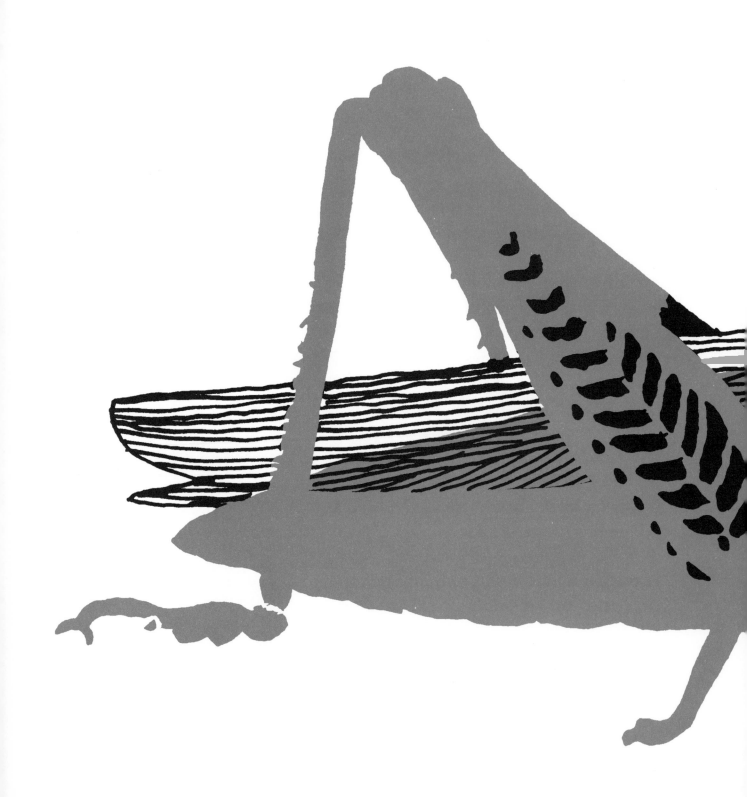

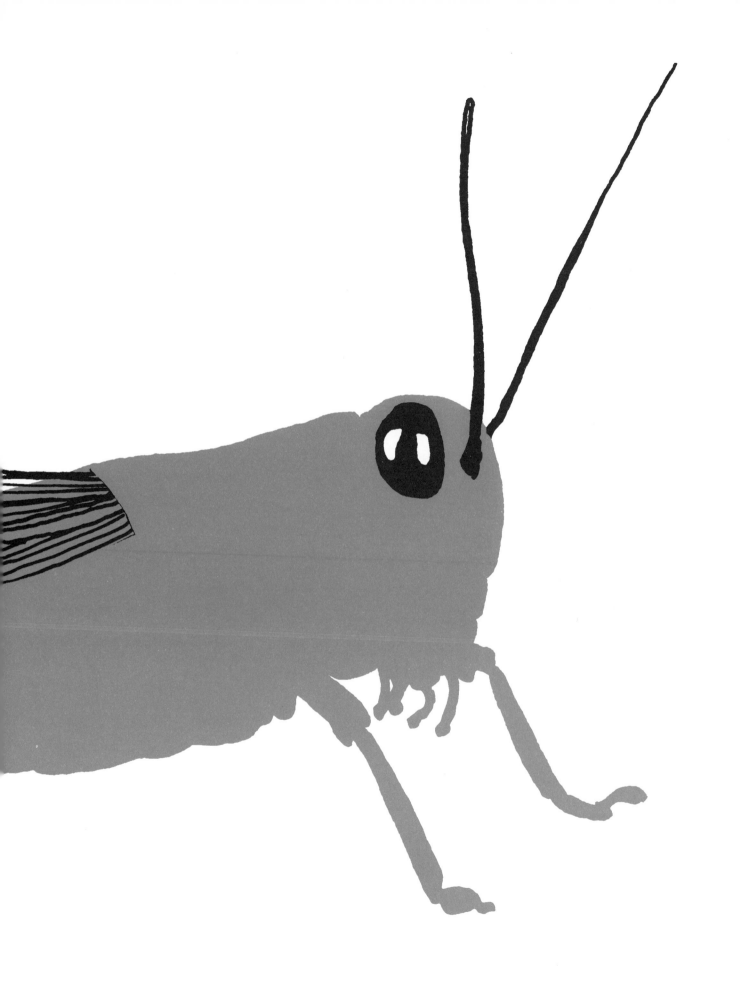

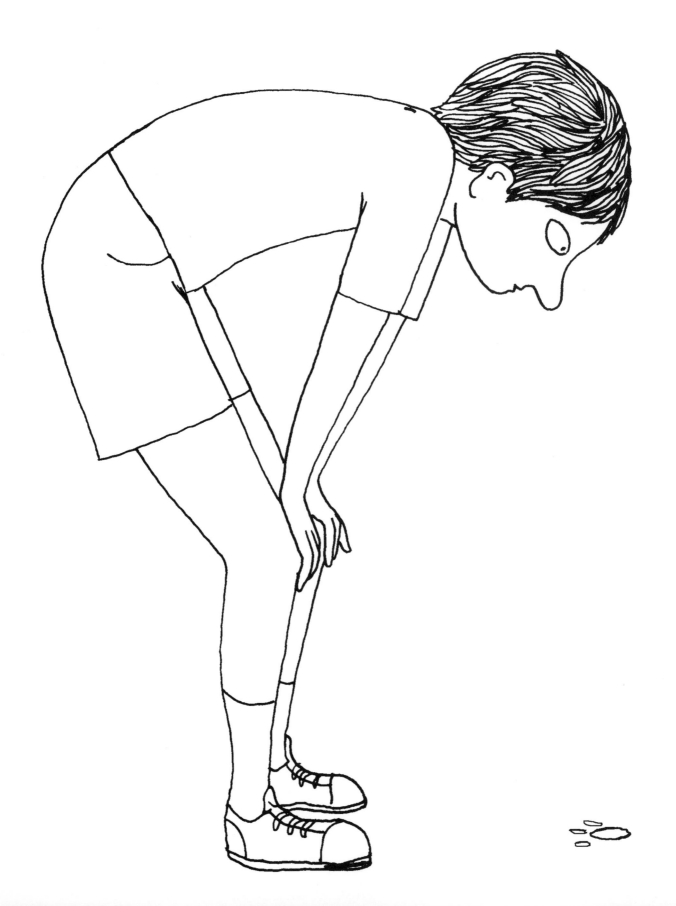

FOLLOW THE CLUES!

THE SIGNS ANIMALS LEAVE BEHIND

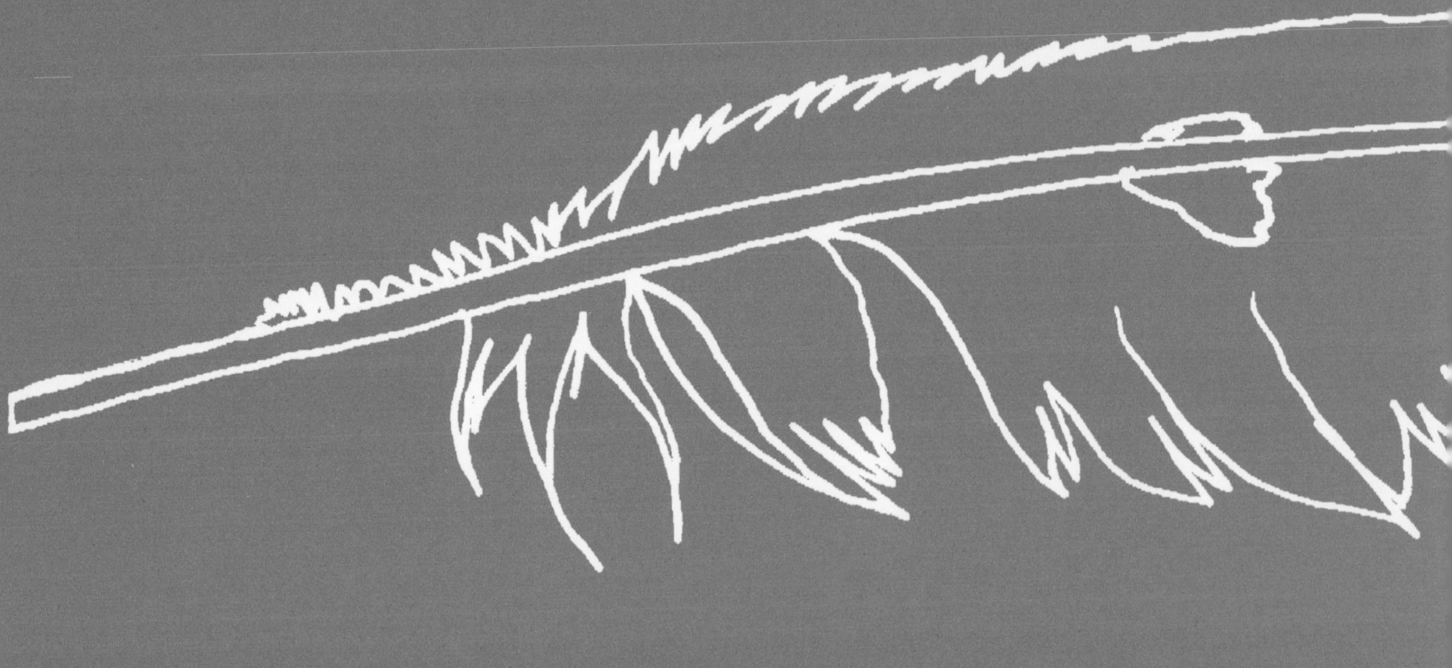

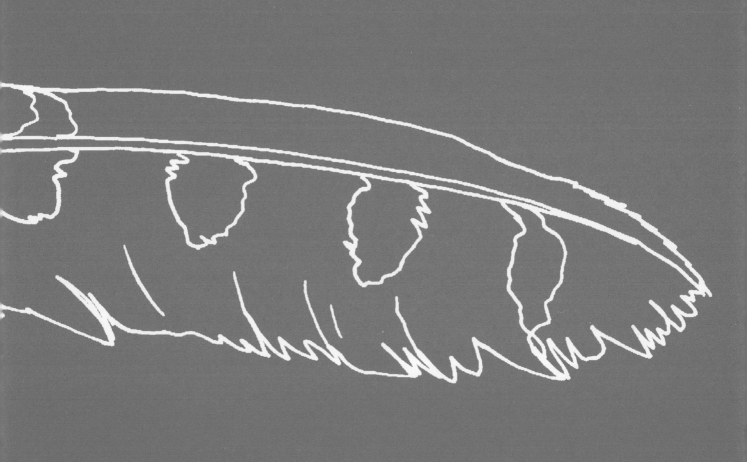

Everyone knows there are all sorts of creatures in the country, but how many of them have you actually seen? The truth is that many of them are hidden and are very hard to find. So how do people manage to study them and find out about their lives?

It's easy—you just have to follow the clues!

What kind of clues do animals leave?

Even though many people don't notice these clues, animals leave a lot of telltale signs behind. It's no wonder, because everything they do in their daily lives—eating, moving, sleeping, reproducing, or growing—leaves some sort of trace we can follow. Ready to investigate?

You are what you eat!

People leave aside bits of food they can't manage to eat, and animals do the same:

<u>Plant-eating animals</u> often leave behind chewed seeds, leaves, or fruits. All these leftovers help us find out exactly which animal was there. Even if there are other animals that eat the same foods, the way they eat is different. You just have to know the signs to look out for.

crossbill

For example, squirrels chew pinecones to get at the pine nuts. They strip off the scales and leave the core. The crossbill likes eating pinecones as well, but it opens them in a different way, so the leftovers look different: the edges of the scales appear ragged, whereas those stripped by a squirrel are cleaner.

<u>Meat-eating animals</u> also leave clues that let us know which has been doing the eating and which was eaten!

For example, many birds of prey eat other birds, leaving their plucked feathers behind. By looking at these feathers, we can find out which bird they belonged to.

eagle

Close-up clues

- - - - - - - - - - - - - - - - - - - -

Pinecones and hazelnuts

If you find a chewed pinecone or hazelnut, try to figure out which animal it belonged to. Look at them carefully and compare them with these pictures.

This pinecone has been frayed and scratched by a woodpecker.

- - - - - - - - -

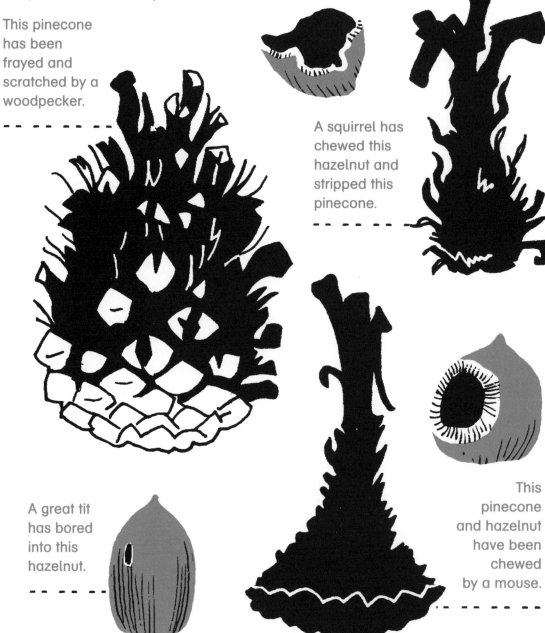

A squirrel has chewed this hazelnut and stripped this pinecone.

- - - - - - - - -

A great tit has bored into this hazelnut.

- - - - - - -

This pinecone and hazelnut have been chewed by a mouse.

- - - - - - - -

Feathers

- - -- -- - -- -- -- -- -- -- - --

Types of feathers

When you find a feather, before trying to figure out which bird it belongs to, you can identify what kind of feather it is.

Flight feathers can be found on the wings and tail of a bird and are unmistakable because they're longer than other feathers and have a hard central shaft (rachis). Two types of flight feathers are shown here: the tail feathers are symmetric, while the wing feathers are asymmetrically shaped.

Contour feathers cover the rest of a bird's body. They also have a central shaft, but it's not as hard as the one in flight feathers. Contour feathers give the bird its smooth shape.

Down feathers are soft, fluffy feathers found underneath the other feathers. They don't have much of a central shaft, and their job is to keep the bird warm.

Which bird?

The shapes and markings of different feathers will help you figure out which birds they came from.

Owl feathers are very soft to the touch, especially the top part of the wing feathers.

With a bit of luck, you might also find **jay feathers,** many of which have striped patterns.

If you live in a city, you will often come across **pigeon feathers,** which are normally small and white, black, or gray.

25

Better out than in!

Unlike the animals we've already talked about (which only eat what they can or what they like), there are others that swallow their prey whole and, after digestion, vomit the parts they're unable to digest. This is the case with the barn owl, which throws up small balls made from the bones and fur of the animals it eats.

Biologists call these balls pellets. They're great clues because they allow us to observe the regurgitated bones, which means we can perhaps figure out which animal they belonged to. With them, we can even assemble the complete skeleton of an animal that has been swallowed!

Animals and their (interesting) feces

Just like when humans eat, there are always parts of food the body rejects when animals eat, and these parts are sent out of the body as feces (the name biologists give to animal poop). In animal feces, we can find everything that wasn't digested, such as seeds, plants, fur, small bones, or insect exoskeletons.

The different shapes, sizes, "ingredients," and smells of feces can tell us what an animal ate, and we can also discover which animal produced it.

Walking, running, slithering

Have you noticed that when you walk barefoot on wet sand, you leave prints that are a perfect copy of your feet? If you rode a bike along the beach, what marks would you leave? Instead of prints, it would be a continuous track, like when you drag a stick along the ground.

The exact same thing happens with animals: the marks they leave on the ground can tell us what species they belong to, if it's an adult or a baby, and if the animal was running or walking.

Feet firmly on the ground

Animals have different legs and move in different ways. And, just like us, they can run, jump, hop, or simply walk. The number of legs each animal has can therefore give us lots of clues:

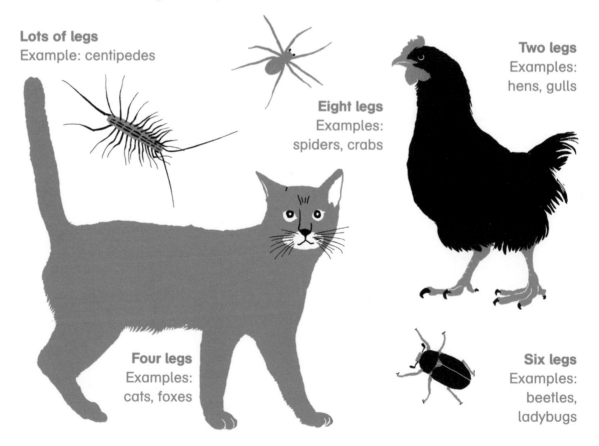

Lots of legs
Example: centipedes

Eight legs
Examples:
spiders, crabs

Two legs
Examples:
hens, gulls

Four legs
Examples:
cats, foxes

Six legs
Examples:
beetles,
ladybugs

Important footprints clues

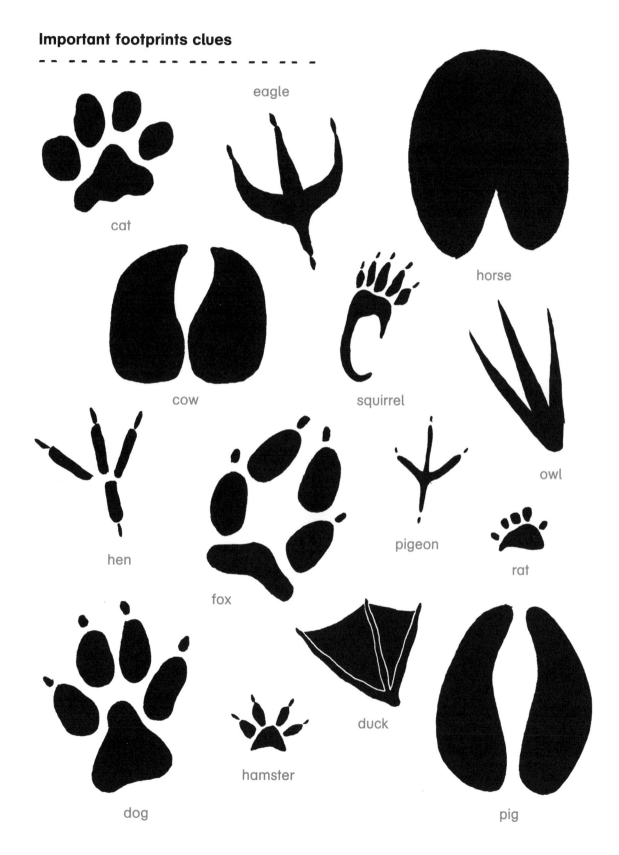

cat

eagle

horse

cow

squirrel

hen

fox

owl

pigeon

rat

dog

hamster

duck

pig

Slithering like a snake

Because they don't have legs, snakes leave very different tracks than other animals. When you find these marks, they are easy to identify.

Important snake track clues

- -

There are five main types of movement along the ground. Some of these movements are used more by certain species, but they can also vary with the condition of the ground: for example, if the ground is sandy or earthy, if the snake can move freely, or if there is little space around it.

1. Rectilinear: Made in open spaces by very big snakes, like the big constrictor species (e.g., anaconda).

4. Concertina: Often used to move through tight spaces, such as tunnels.

5. Lateral undulation: The most common among many species.

2. Lateral slide: One of the most well-known tracks. Corresponds to tracks on sand and other slippery surfaces, such as those left by snakes in the desert.

3. Jumps:

Always on the same path

There are animals that tend to take the same route somewhere (like you when you go to school each day). This means a path gets marked on the ground. If it's a big animal, a wide path is formed; if it's a small animal, a narrower path is formed.

Mammals are usually more difficult to see than birds, but fortunately they leave a lot of clues! Almost all of them leave tracks that we can identify:

- Just as their name suggests, water voles love water. To get there, they make a network of footpaths through the grass to better protect themselves from predators. These paths are about 4 in (10 cm) wide.
- Badgers (animals much larger than water voles) also leave paths in the places where they walk many times. These paths, which are about 12 in (30 cm) wide, lead to the entrances of their dens.

Become an animal detective in the country!

- -

The edge of a river is an excellent place to see tracks because lots of animals go there to drink water, eat, or even take a dip!

Tips:

- To watch animals, you have to be cautious and silent, because otherwise your presence will scare them. Talk quietly, and communicate with your friends using gestures.

- Don't try to interfere with the animals you're watching. Don't give them food, don't try to "help them," and leave their nests or burrows alone.

✳

Become an animal detective in the city!

- -

Discover them all around!

Tips:

- You can take photographs or draw the footprints that you find. That way it's easier to study the shapes and spot the differences.

- Never touch animal excrement, because it might give you diseases. This is a job only for biologists, and must be done with the right equipment.

exuvias

Comfortable in your own skin!

Just like us, all other animals grow. There are some that never stop growing, even when they're really old, like octopuses, lobsters, or corals (they don't look like it, but corals are animals). Unlike our skin, some other animals' skins don't grow, which means their "owners" start to feel very squeezed inside it. That means it's time to undress!

Some examples

When animals "take off" their skin, they often leave it in the middle of the path, and that can be a great clue for us.

Among the animals that get "undressed" are snakes, which leave their old skin as if they're turning a sock inside out: they rub their bodies along the ground and vegetation until their skin comes off whole!

If you're lucky enough to find a snakeskin, you can try to see which part is the head. This is the part that lets you identify the snake down to its species.

There are other animals that change their skin, such as grasshoppers (in this case, it's not a "skin" but rather an exoskeleton, which is the name for a skeleton on the outside of the body). When they come out of the egg, grasshoppers are called nymphs and have a white exoskeleton. These nymphs grow, and at a certain size, they have to change the exoskeleton because they no longer fit inside it. That's why you can sometimes find these white exoskeletons (called exuvias) in the country or in a yard.

Common
kingsnake,
Lampropeltis getula

Grass snake (juvenile)

Natrix natrix

Smooth snake

Coronella austriaca

Short-headed gartersnake

Thamnophis sirtalis

Western rattlesnake

Crotalus oreganus

36

Snakes are special because they shed
their skins in one go, unlike other
animals, whose skin comes off in pieces.
You can tell if a snake is about to shed
when its skin looks dull and its
eyes go a cloudy blueish color.

Copperhead
Agkistrodon contortrix

Northern water snake
Nerodia sipedon

Adder
Vipera berus

Home, sweet home . . .

However much we like wandering around outside, there comes a time when we want to go home. Maybe because it's very cold, or it's going to rain, or we're tired and all we can think about is sleeping in our beds. The same happens with animals, or at least something similar.

Animals have houses different than ours (even if some live in our houses without us realizing) and their nests and burrows are also great clues.

Nests in the trees
There are lots of birds that make nests in the trees, like starlings—birds that are common almost everywhere and lay blue eggs. There are also mammals that make nests in trees, like dormice, which take advantage of openings and holes in trees to make their homes.

There are lots of different ways to make nests (you'll find more information on this topic in the "Birds" chapter).

Some prefer to have their houses underground
You might have already seen several heaps of soil close to one another in the country or in a yard. Have you ever thought what they might be?

To protect themselves, there are lots of animals that make burrows underneath the ground (and when they make these burrows, they leave soil outside, of course). These are excellent clues for us!

Now you know: holes in the ground or heaps of soil are a sign that somebody is down there making tunnels. These might be, for example, moles or voles.

There are clues to follow everywhere, so get going! You can look for clues on the beach, in the country, and even in the city.

Garden dormouse

BUT WHAT KIND OF BUG CAN THIS BE?

BUGS AND CRITTERS

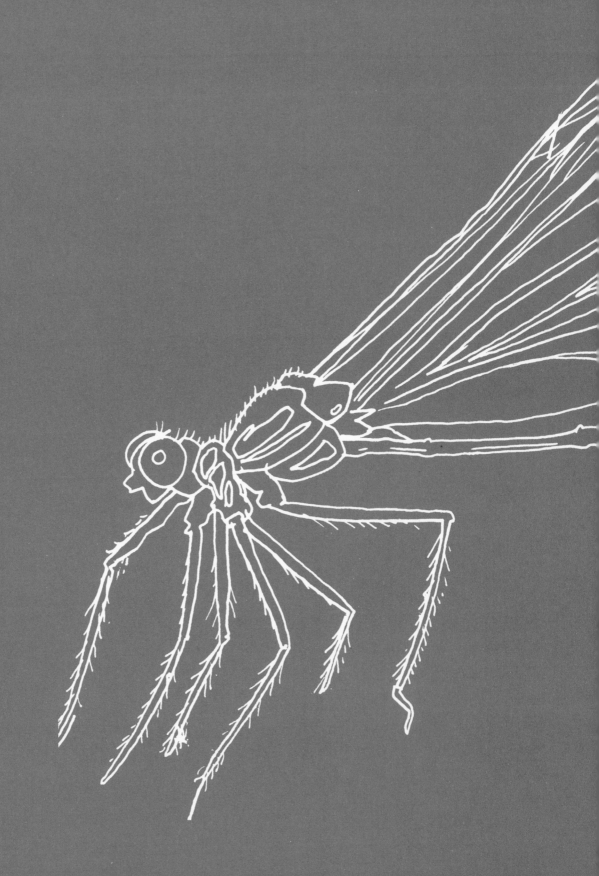

Not all animals are rare or hard to find. There are lots of bugs, creepy-crawlies, and critters that are very easy to spot and that we come across quite often, while they're climbing a wall, wandering across the ground in front of us, or fluttering around.

Worms, slugs, ants, butterflies, and snails: welcome to this book!

Let's start with worms . . .

All species of segmented worms have moist skin and a long, soft, tubelike body made of segments, or rings. It is these rings that give worms their special powers. What kind of powers, you ask?

When they lose one of their segments, these worms (like all annelids) can regrow it, an ability that is very useful. Imagine, for example, a robin pecks a worm: if the bird takes away a part of the worm's body, the worm is able to regenerate and survive.

Leeches and polychaetes are also annelids. Most leeches live in shallow freshwater and feed off the blood of other animals. Polychaetes are similar to worms, but they live in water. People often use them as bait for fishing.

Are there male and female worms?

No . . . and yes. Worms are hermaphrodites, which means they are male and female at the same time. Even though they have two sexes, a single worm cannot reproduce alone. It always has to find another worm, and after the two of them come together to reproduce, both can lay eggs.

Do worms have a heart?

Worms don't just have one heart—they have several! And some Australian species of worm are so long, growing up to 10 ft (3 m) in length, that they need 15 hearts to pump blood through their bodies.

The best way to learn about worms is by looking at them. Shall we?

● I caught a worm!

Worms like soil that's moist and not too hard, like the soil you find in most vegetable gardens. If you know somebody who has a vegetable garden, you can ask them if they often see worms (it's always a good idea to ask someone with experience). When you find a place with loose, moist soil, try digging a bit to look for worms. You can do this with a small spade or a trowel, or even with your hands. (If you don't want to get dirty, you can use gardening gloves.)

Tips:

● If the soil is very dry, wet it with a bit of water.

● Take a bucket and put a some soil inside it. You can put worms into the bucket for observation.

● Be careful when you dig so you don't cut any worms in half.

● Use the worms you collect to do the experiments we suggest on the following pages.

Look at worms through a magnifying glass

- - - - - - - - - - - - - - -

Place a worm on a piece of thick paper or cardstock. Wait for the worm to start moving across the paper.

Get close and try to hear the noise the setae make as the worm slides across the paper. Notice the way the worm's body contorts: that's the muscles contracting.

Run your hand over it slowly to feel the rings. If you've got a magnifying glass, you'll be able to better see all the details of its body.

- - - - - - - - - - - - -

How can worms move if they don't have legs?
On each of the segments of a worm's body, there are four pairs of tiny bristly hairs called setae. When worms move, they contort their muscles and the setae help, as if they were little legs.

Do the experiment on this page, and you'll be able to observe this.

Do worms have noses?

Worms don't have what we would usually call a nose, nor do they have lungs, because they use their skin to absorb the oxygen that is dissolved in damp soil. When it rains a lot and the soil gets full of water, there is no more oxygen and worms have to come to the surface to breathe.

Prove that worms have a special nose by doing the activity suggested on the right.

What do worms *do*?

It might not seem like it, but worms are very useful:

- <u>Lots of animals eat worms,</u> like robins, blackbirds, salamanders, badgers, and moles.
- <u>Worms eat the remains of animals and plants and turn these remains into nutrients.</u> These nutrients end up in the worms' poop (called castings), which is left behind in the soil, and then these nutrients can be used by plants. Worms are very important for fertilizing soil!
- <u>Worms make a lot of tunnels, which let air and water into the soil, and this allows plants to get more nutrients.</u>

Today there are factories where the workers are worms! What they do there is called vermicomposting. It's a strange name, but pretty simple: the worms turn organic waste (like food waste) into fertilizer for the soil.

Prove that worms have a special nose

- - - - - - - - - - - - - - - - -

Put a worm on a damp cloth. Soak a cotton ball in acetone (ask an adult for help) and move it close to the worm's head, without touching the worm!

Now do the same at the other end of the worm and along its side. Notice how the worm reacts the same all over its body. This is because the worm smells the acetone in all its segments. In other words, its whole body is one big nose!

- - - - - - - - - - - - - - - - -

Let's follow slugs and snails

How are slugs and snails related?
Both belong to a group called mollusks,
the same group that includes octopuses,
cuttlefish, squid, mussels, cowries, clams,
and many others.

**If they look so different, how can
they all be mollusks?**
Because they're all invertebrates, and
they all have soft bodies without
segments or rings. Many mollusks'
bodies are divided into three
parts: head, visceral mass,
and foot (see illustration).

**Why do snails carry their
houses on their backs?**
Snails hide inside their shells
so they don't get eaten by
predators. When it's hot
out, the shell also
protects their skin
and prevents them
from drying out
and dying.

Just like our bones, snails'
shells are made of calcium.

Visceral mass: The
internal organs (e.g., heart
and lungs) are found
underneath the shell.

Foot: This is a very strong
muscle and is the part
that touches the ground.

Head: This is where the eyes and tentacles are found.

Why don't slugs have shells?

It's a well-kept secret, but most slugs do have shells—it's just that it's a small shell inside their body that lost its protective function thousands of years ago. No one knows exactly why slugs and other mollusks evolved to not have a shell or to have a reduced shell inside their body, but we think it was probably so they can explore other habitats better. Because a snail goes everywhere with its house on its back, it's certainly more difficult for it to get into tight places or go underneath logs or stones. Slugs, meanwhile, can easily slip through any crack, compressing their bodies and getting into places snails can't.

● **Look for snail shells**

- -

Where: Near fences or stuck to posts.
- Notice the different types and textures of shells (are they wrinkled or smooth?).
- Organize them by size: younger snails have smaller shells (as the snail grows, the shell grows, too).
- And finally, look which way the shells twist (left or right?). If all the spirals go the same way, then it's possible that they belong to the same species.

- -

Geomalacus maculosus

Look at bugs through a magnifying glass

Bugs are almost always tiny little things. With the help of a magnifying glass, you can get a better look at their details: texture and colors, eyes, legs, antennae, and tentacles (if they have them).

Look carefully and draw all the details you discover.

Plagues or rare bugs?

Often, gardens are infested by a plague of snails, with countless snails eating all the plants they come across. However, there are species that are in danger of extinction, despite how easily they reproduce. This is the case with *Actinella carinofausta*, a species unique to the island of Madeira in Portugal.

The slug *Geomalacus maculosus* only lives in Portugal, Spain, and Ireland and is protected by conservation laws. When it feels threatened, it rolls up completely into a ball-like shape, an unusual characteristic in the world of slugs.

Do snails have teeth?

Snails mainly eat plants, but they can also eat other snails and even bird poop! Slugs also eat plants, mosses, and fungi, but some can be carnivorous, eating other slugs, snails, worms, and the remains of other animals.

Inside their mouths, both snails and slugs have a radula, which looks like a grater made from hard rubber. On the radula, there are rows and rows of tiny teeth that break up food so it can be swallowed.

Why do snails and slugs always leave slime?

We already know that snails and slugs are both mollusks, and they have something else in common: slime! They leave it wherever they go.

This slime is called mucus. Let's take a look at it and see what it does . . .

● **Look at snail and slug slime**

- -

When?
After it's rained. Slugs and snails like moisture.

Where?
You can find snails and slugs under logs and stones in a yard, garden, or open space.

Tips:

- If you have a magnifying glass, take it with you.

- Stay still while you wait and watch snails move. Notice how slowly they move and how they leave slime on the ground as they move. This slime helps them move on smooth surfaces, such as leaves, without slipping.

- Slugs can produce two types of mucus (which can even be different colors): one that helps them move and another that protects their skin so it doesn't dry out.

- If it's hot, try putting a snail on a smooth, dry surface, such as a cement floor. Notice how the mucus that the snail leaves on the ground doesn't make a continuous line, but leaves gaps. The snail is able to place its foot so it loses the least amount of mucus possible and therefore doesn't dehydrate.

- -

Where are the eyes?

Slugs and snails have two pairs of tentacles on their heads. The eyes are on the upper tentacles, and the lower ones are used for smelling. Both are retractable, which means they can be pulled in. And if they're ever cut off, they can grow right back.

Do you believe in Cupid?

You might not, but he exists . . . in the form of a snail.

When a snail wants to mate with another snail, it gets up close and pricks it with a kind of dart. This dart contains substances that increase the chances of fertilizing the chosen snail—it is called a gypsobelum, or a love dart.

Just like worms, slugs and snails are hermaphrodites. When two of them reproduce, both can lay eggs: they make a hole in the ground and lay the eggs there, normally several dozen eggs. When they hatch, the snails are already wearing their shells!

● **How many legs?**

- -

Whenever you see a bug, count how many legs it has. Beetles, like this one here, have three legs on each side of their body.

If you find a creepy-crawly with six legs, you know that it's an insect. Ladybugs, grasshoppers, ants, and cockroaches all have six legs. But even though they have the same number of legs, one insect's legs can be very different than the legs of another. (See the opposite page for some different kinds of legs.)

- -

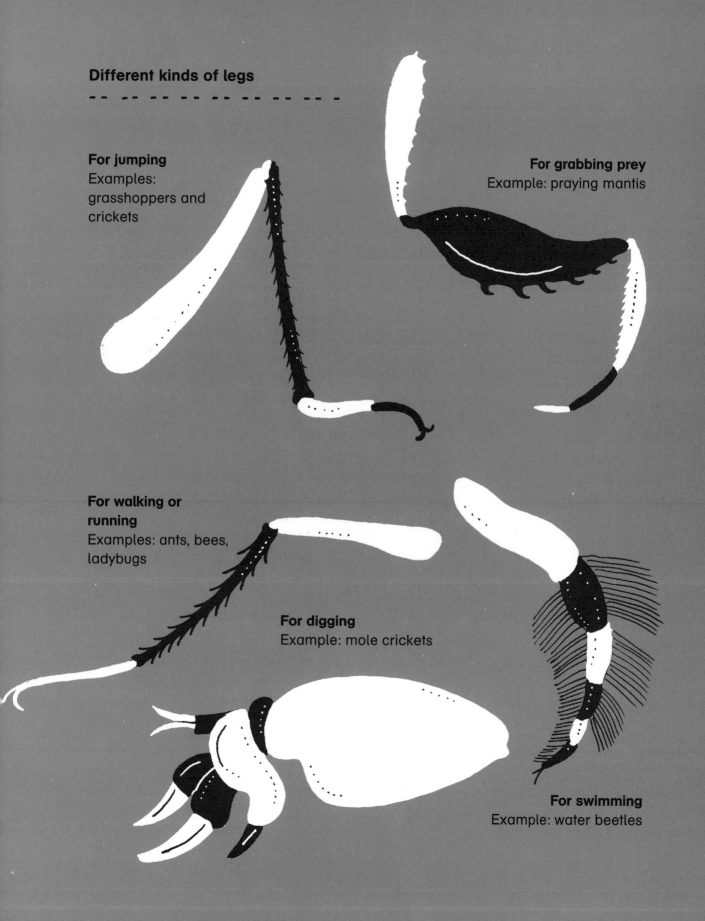

Different kinds of legs

For jumping
Examples: grasshoppers and crickets

For grabbing prey
Example: praying mantis

For walking or running
Examples: ants, bees, ladybugs

For digging
Example: mole crickets

For swimming
Example: water beetles

Go out at night and watch fireflies

Fireflies like dark places because they communicate using a language made of glowing lights. (And if there's a lot of light out, the other fireflies can't see the messages they're trying to send.)

Where to look?
You are most likely to find fireflies in areas with a lot of natural vegetation. (However, you can also find fireflies in a yard or garden.)

Look for them in the most hidden (and the darkest) places, in vegetation close to the ground.

When?
Fireflies can only be seen at the end of spring and in the summer. But still, sometimes it's not too easy to find them.

You know what to do—look for them in the dark!

An interesting fact: Did you know that the eggs of some species of fireflies are also luminous?

Ants and other insects

Insects are one of the most abundant groups of animals on our planet.

There are so many insects around the world that scientists can't decide how many species there are in total. (Some say there are 5 million; others think there are 100 million). So far, we know of almost one million species, but who knows how many more there are.

Unlike some animals we've already discussed, insects are tougher because they have a covering on the outside of their bodies. Because it's hard and outside the body's muscles, this covering is called an exoskeleton, which means a skeleton on the outside of the body.

Because there are so many of them and because they are all around us, insects are some of the easiest animals to find.
Shall we take a look?

Little ant, where are you?

- - - - - - - - - - - - - - - - - - - -

Go out onto the sidewalk searching for ants. Look for them on the trunks of trees, on plants, or in the soil. Because they're so small, you'll have to pay close attention.

When you find an ant, look at it closely. All ants are smooth and normally dark-colored: black, brown, or dark red. Unlike worms or snails, which have soft and sticky-looking skin, ants have harder bodies. Now you know it's their exoskeletons that make them look like that.

Why do ants touch each other with their antennae?

Ants' antennae are articulated, which means that they're made up of several pieces joined together. The main function of the ants' antennae is to pick up smells. Every ant has two antennae, which helps them determine the direction a smell is coming from.

When two ants meet, they touch antennae to pick up the other's scents, and this is how they communicate. For example, if an ant is hungry, it tells the other one by giving off a certain smell. This smell can even "ask" the other other ant to regurgitate food for it to eat. It may seem like a strange snack, but not for an ant.

Lots of other insects have antennae, and normally the main function is the same: to smell. There are species, like certain moths, that have such big antennae that they're able to pick up smells from miles away!

Feed an anthill

Spread little pieces of bread, cookies, or fruit (cut up very small) in the area around the anthill. Sit back and watch the ants have a feast!
Be careful: Don't leave food inside the anthill or block the entrance!

Draw a map of the anthill

Follow the ants when they come out of the anthill, marking the route they take. Plot the paths around the anthill, including the biggest obstacles for the ants (normally the path takes a detour and doesn't go over them) as well as any other entrances you come across.

What's life like in an anthill?

Ants live in a very organized society, which means that each type of ant has a different job in the anthill.

Living in an anthill, you will usually find:
- a <u>queen</u> **(1)**, which is normally bigger than the other ants and lays eggs constantly throughout her life;
- the <u>workers</u> **(2)**, which are females responsible for maintaining and defending the anthill;
- in some anthills, <u>soldiers</u> **(3)**, which are bigger and stronger and defend the anthill from invaders;
- the <u>males</u> **(4)**, which have a reproductive role.

An anthill is divided into various chambers, which are sort of like rooms. In the <u>pantry</u> **(5)**, the ants store seeds and other food, such as decomposing leaves. Do you know why? Because on these leaves, some species of ant grow fungi that they eat.

In the <u>nursery</u> **(6)**, the workers look after the larvae that will become baby ants. In the <u>storeroom</u> **(7)**, which is found at the bottom of the anthill, the ants store garbage (e.g., remains of leaves and dead ants); they care a lot about hygiene. In an anthill, there can also be <u>traps</u> **(8)**, false tunnels to make potential invaders waste time if they attack the anthill.

Why do some ants have wings?

Only the reproductive ants (female and male) are born with wings, and at a certain stage, thousands of them fly out of the anthill for their nuptial flight, to reproduce and to form new anthills. After copulation, they lose their wings. Then the females become new queens and the males die. The wings are only used by the ants to move to new places, far away from their anthill, and start everything again!

Look for different types of ants

- - - - - - - - - - - - - -

It'll be difficult to see the queen because she's very well protected inside the anthill. But you can try and find soldier ants and worker ants. You'll see that the soldiers have bigger heads and mouthparts and stay close to the entrance of the anthill.

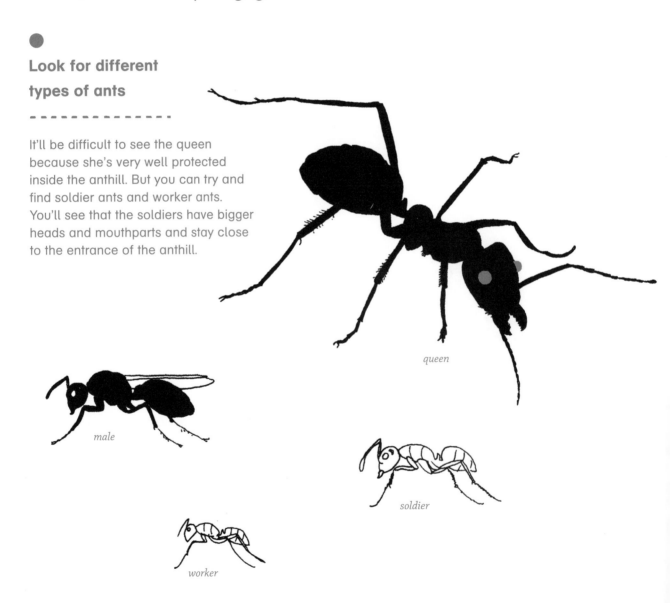

queen

male

soldier

worker

62

Is it true that in summer while the ants work, the cicadas sing?
It is technically true that ants spend the summer working, while the cicadas sing, but this doesn't mean that one is hardworking and the other's lazy! Only adult male cicadas sing, to attract females. If the females like the song, they come close so they can reproduce. (Everything in nature has a function!)

Some cicadas sing so loudly that they're able to wake us up at night, and there are some species whose song is so sharp that, even though it's not perceptible to the human ear, it can make some dogs howl in pain! Cicadas even have to protect themselves from their own singing: both males and females have eardrums shaped in a way that the sound doesn't cause internal damage.

If you try to capture a cicada and it flies away, you'll see that it leaves a liquid behind. It's not urine—it's just water or sap. Some biologists think that when cicadas flee, they get rid of some weight to make themselves lighter and more agile.

● **Use colors to attract insects**

- -

You can try this trick to attract insects:

Put colored plates (yellow, blue, red) in the sun, with a few drops of water in them. Then sit down and watch the insects that arrive, attracted by the colors and by the water.

Where?
In a garden, yard, or in the country.

When?
Choose a sunny spring day.

cicada

- -

Why do ants almost never leave the path?

Ants communicate with one another using chemical substances called pheromones. For example, when an ant finds food, it has to take it to the anthill and also tell the other ants about the location of the food so they can go and bring back the rest of it. The ant leaves pheromones along the way so that the others can follow. As more and more ants go to that place, more pheromones are left. The more ants that go there, the stronger the smell becomes and the more ants it will attract. Do you know why ants all walk in single file? It's because they're following each other's smell.

Intruders

As we've already seen, ants have everything they need inside the anthill: a nursery for the larvae, pantries with food, the queen's room, and even, just imagine, a trash can.

●● ●

Write a diary of the life of an ant

- - - - - - - - - - - - - - -

Sit next to an anthill and watch what happens: ants and their "deliveries" going in and out, as well as what goes on all around the anthill. You can watch the anthill and the ants for a few minutes or throughout a whole week, and note down the changes. (Imagine if it rains—what would happen?)

Look at the ants' paths

- - - - - - - - - - - - - - -

Find an anthill or an ant's path. Look at the way the ants walk; they hardly ever leave the path. Also notice how the ants touch each other's antennae when they pass each other. Try an experiment, and put a piece of food that ants like (they prefer sweet things) just off the path. Now wait to see what happens . . . Will the ants find their way to your treat?

Anthills are warm and cozy in the winter and cool and airy in the summer. Because anthills are so comfortable, other insects want to live there. And sometimes they do.

Some of these intruders are <u>broad-headed bugs</u> (1), <u>beetles</u> (2), <u>flies</u> (3), <u>moths</u> (4), and <u>spiders</u> (5). These animals disguise themselves using the scent of ants so the ants won't attack them. And where do they get this scent?

Most intruders in anthills can naturally imitate the smells and behavior of ants. Other species can extract chemical substances from the wax that covers the bodies of dead ants, and then spread it over their own bodies. This way, when an ant walks past them, the ant doesn't even notice that these insects don't belong in the anthill.

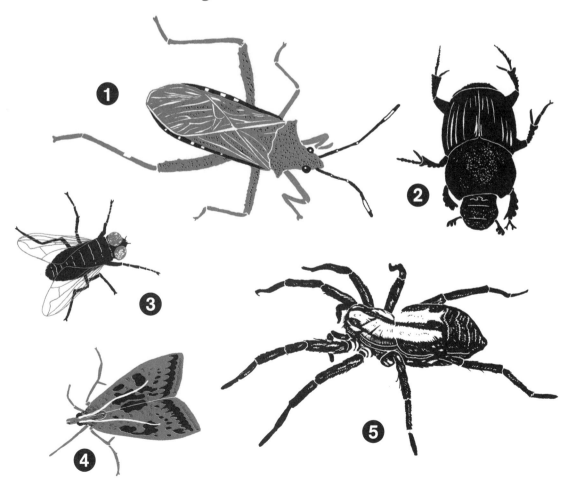

Butterflies

If you manage to get close enough to a butterfly to count its legs, you'll see that there are six, as with all insects. You'll also be able to appreciate its amazing body.

Butterflies with <u>large wings</u> (1) can glide long distances without flapping very often. Those with smaller wings have to beat them faster—some up to 80 times per second.

A butterfly's <u>eyes</u> (2) are made up of thousands of tiny lenses. Still, butterflies can't see very clearly and are unable to detect slow movements.

Some species of butterfly have "<u>ears</u> " (3) at the base of their wings, which allow them to hear birds or other hunters. A butterfly's feelers, or <u>antennae</u> (4), work like a nose to help it find food. They stick out from its body so it can sense which direction different smells are coming from. They also help the butterfly balance.

The mouth is a tube called a proboscis. It works like a straw, allowing the butterfly to suck up nectar from flowers. When the butterfly is resting, the proboscis stays rolled up, but it when it drinks it unfurls . . . sluuurp!

And how does a butterfly get its incredible colors? From the pigments of the plants that it ate when it was just a caterpillar.

How is a butterfly born?

- - - - - - - - -

Butterflies lay eggs. From an egg comes a caterpillar that eats a lot, growing bigger and bigger. Then it sheds its skin to reveal a case underneath called a chrysalis, or pupa. Inside the chrysalis, the caterpillar changes, and a brand-new butterfly emerges! This kind of transformation is called a metamorphosis.

Go out to look at butterflies

When?
The best time of year for observing butterflies is between March and September, because these are the months when there are more flowers and more sunlight—butterflies' favorite things! Choose a day when it isn't windy, since butterflies are sensitive insects. The best time of day is between 11 a.m. and 4 p.m.

Where?
Try walking anywhere that there are flowers, and look carefully.

What to do?
When you see a butterfly, first write down what color it is. At the end of your observation, you'll have the number of each color of butterfly. Then, later, you can investigate which species are the colors you saw more of, and you might come to some conclusions.

To help you, look for the butterfly species page in the center of the book.

IS IT A FROG

OR A TOAD?

AMPHIBIANS

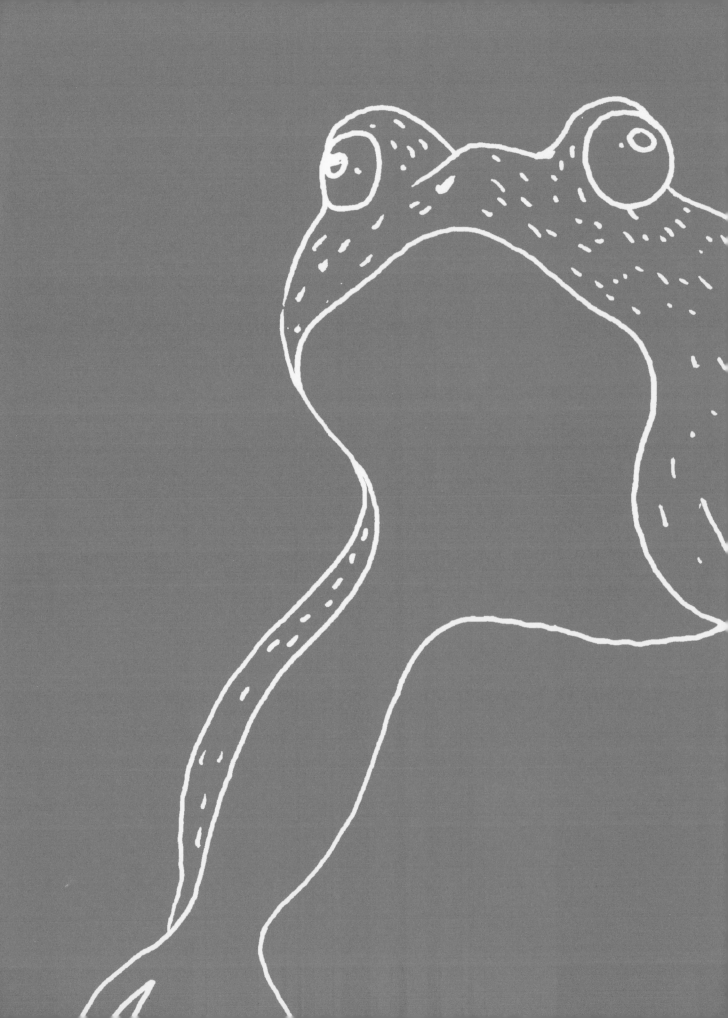

Do you hear that?
Those're toads, right?
(Or are they frogs?)
Do toads make noise on summer nights?
Do they try to outsing one another?
Do they sing their tadpoles to sleep?

**Shall we go outside to see if we can
hear them?**

Amphibian? What kind of animal is that?

The word amphibian comes from the ancient Greek *amphibios*, which means "two lives." But do amphibians really have two lives? Maybe . . . When they're really small, frogs and toads are tadpoles, and they live in the water, where they breathe through gills like fish. But when they grow, they lose their tails, their gills become lungs, and they go live on land. It's like they do actually have two lives: one in the water and another on land.

Do you want to get to know them better?
A frogs' <u>skin</u> is smooth, without fur or scales. It is also thin and permeable to let water and oxygen through, because frogs mainly breathe through their skin. (Their lungs are very simple and not very efficient.)

Most frogs come out of their hiding places at night, when the temperature is lower and there is no danger of getting exposed to the sun. That way, their skin doesn't dry out so easily!

- -

Did you know that frogs shed their skin like snakes? When the skin gets old, they pull it off with their feet, and sometimes they even eat it.

Frogs' <u>nostrils and eyes</u> are found on the top of their heads, which allows them to keep their bodies in the water, but their eyes and nostrils out.

Frogs and toads have almost always very small teeth and a lot of them don't have teeth at all, but their <u>jaws</u> are strong and help them swallow their food.

Some species are able to stick their <u>tongues</u> out to grab food.

Frogs don't have ears, but they do have <u>eardrums</u> on the outside of their heads. (Look for the round patches in the area behind the eyes.) They have excellent hearing!

Male frogs croak, or make sounds, to attract females during mating season. To croak, they fill their <u>vocal sacs</u> (the "pouches" under their chins) with air.

Some species are able to jump 20 times farther than their own length. This is because they have special <u>legs</u>: their back legs are much longer than their front legs, which helps them get their balance when jumping. It also makes them look like they're always sitting down.

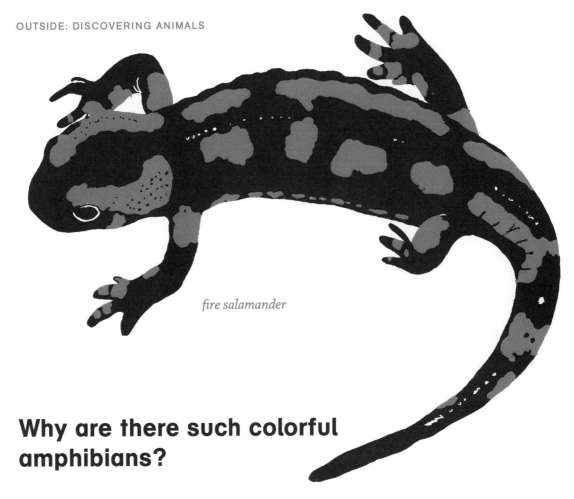

fire salamander

Why are there such colorful amphibians?

Some amphibians are colorful to attract attention. The colors are used to warn predators: "These colors mean I'm not at all tasty—I'm even sort of toxic!"

Fire salamanders, which are all black with yellow spots (sometimes red), release toxic substances from their parotid glands (the raised parts on their heads behind their eyes). A snake would eat a salamander and vomit it right back up . . . it made him feel sick!

Some substances released by amphibians are not poisonous, but they can irritate our eyes. That's why you should always wash your hands after you touch an amphibian.

Where do these toxic substances come from?

- - - - - - - - --

Almost all of them originate from the insects that amphibians eat.

Curious amphibians

- - - - - - - - - - - - - -

The biggest amphibian in the world is the Chinese giant salamander, which can grow up to 6 ft (2 m) long!

The smallest amphibian in the world is a tiny frog that lives in the forests of Papua New Guinea and measures only .30 in (7.7 mm) (its scientific name is *Paedophryne amauensis).* It is also the smallest vertebrate in the world.

The genus name for midwife toads, *Alytes,* comes from the Latin *Allium,* which means "garlic." That's because when they're disturbed, they leave a strong smell of garlic.

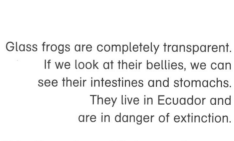

Glass frogs are completely transparent. If we look at their bellies, we can see their intestines and stomachs. They live in Ecuador and are in danger of extinction.

Reinette apples got their name because their peel looks like toad skin (reinette comes from the Latin word *rana,* meaning "frog").

One of the strongest poisons in the world comes from a small frog in the Amazon rainforest, and it is used by indigenous people for hunting. For a guaranteed result, it's enough for them to simply touch the tips of their arrows on this frog's back.

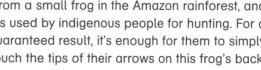

But if they taste so bad . . .

What would want to eat them?

Even though they taste "bad," amphibians have lots of predators:

- Water snakes **(1)** eat toads **(2)** and frogs **(3)** when they're still tadpoles **(4)**;
- Freshwater fish **(5)** also eat lots of amphibian larvae **(6)** (and can even cause their extinction in some places);
- other animals like storks **(7)**, barn owls **(8)**, and polecats **(9)** also like to eat amphibians.

And do you know what else? Other amphibians! One fire salamander will eat another fire salamander! Yikes!

And speaking of food . . .

-- -- -- -- -- --

Do you know what amphibians eat?

Amphibians are mainly carnivores, which means they eat other animals: spiders, worms, insects, etc. But when they're still larvae (tadpoles), frogs and toads are mainly herbivores.

-- -- -- -- -- --

All amphibians, but different

In many places around the world, there are only two types of amphibians: anura and urodela.

In some tropical countries, there is a third type called apoda (amphibians that don't have a tail or legs and look a bit like worms).

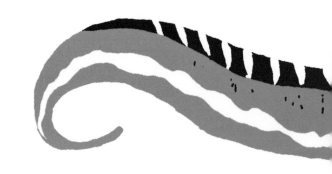

How to tell anura and urodela apart

- - - - - - - - - - - - - - - - - - -

Anura don't have tails. Their back legs are bigger than their front legs, so they have to stay doubled up, which means that these animals look like they're always sitting down. Examples: toads, frogs, and tree frogs.

tree frog

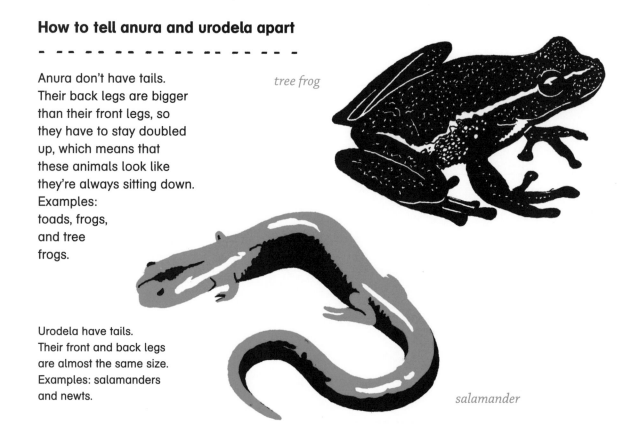

Urodela have tails. Their front and back legs are almost the same size. Examples: salamanders and newts.

salamander

marbled newt

Some dance and others sing, but all for romance!

When it comes to finding a partner to mate with, amphibians are different: frogs and toads prefer to sing, while newts and salamanders prefer to dance a few steps.

Every species of toad or frog has a special song to attract a mate. Following lots of rain on spring and autumn nights, we can often hear males singing in the hope of attracting a female.

In the dances of salamanders and newts, males chase the females and dance in front of them with repetitive movements.

Salamanders do their dance on land. All other species of urodela do their dance in water, which makes it more difficult for us to see.

In many species, the males become better looking during mating season: they can become more colorful or develop crests on their backs, like marbled newts do.

Catch frogs

- - - - - - - - - - - - - - - - - -

During spring and summer, you can use a net to try to catch frogs from a nearby marsh or riverbank.

You might catch frogs as well as newts, tadpoles, salamanders, and small water insects.

Remember to return them to nature after you've observed them.

Don't forget:
Frogs are cold-blooded animals, which means that some species have to hibernate in winter to survive. Some also hibernate in summer (which is known as estivation).

- - - - - - - - - - - - - - - - - -

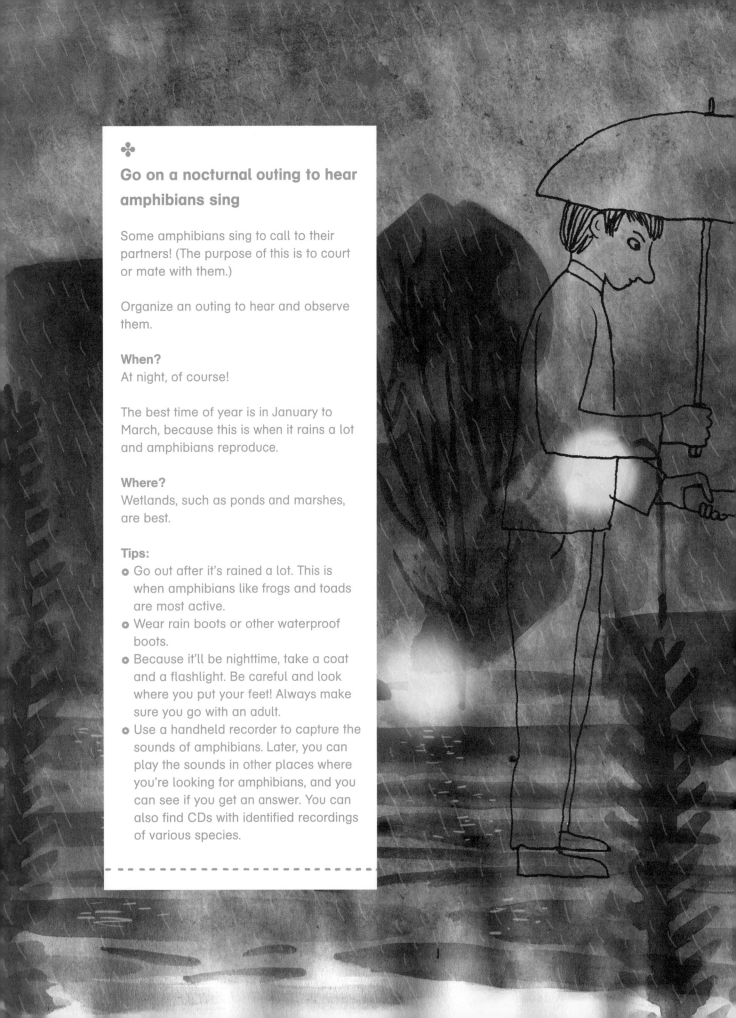

Go on a nocturnal outing to hear amphibians sing

Some amphibians sing to call to their partners! (The purpose of this is to court or mate with them.)

Organize an outing to hear and observe them.

When?
At night, of course!

The best time of year is in January to March, because this is when it rains a lot and amphibians reproduce.

Where?
Wetlands, such as ponds and marshes, are best.

Tips:
- Go out after it's rained a lot. This is when amphibians like frogs and toads are most active.
- Wear rain boots or other waterproof boots.
- Because it'll be nighttime, take a coat and a flashlight. Be careful and look where you put your feet! Always make sure you go with an adult.
- Use a handheld recorder to capture the sounds of amphibians. Later, you can play the sounds in other places where you're looking for amphibians, and you can see if you get an answer. You can also find CDs with identified recordings of various species.

It's not just hens that lay eggs

Almost all amphibians lay eggs as well.

Most frogs, toads, salamanders, and newts are oviparous: they lay eggs, and their young grow inside these eggs until they're ready to come out. Frogs and toads lay eggs in groups; salamanders and newts lay single eggs.

Less common are amphibians that are ovoviviparous, like the fire salamander. This means the egg develops inside the mother's body.

It's possible to identify amphibians from the eggs they lay

- - -- - -- - -- - -- - -- - -

Common parsley frog
It lays dark eggs, wrapped in a transparent gelatinous film, forming very wide, short strands.

Perez's frog and Iberian frog
They lay whitish-brown eggs, wrapped in a transparent gelatinous film, forming a big mass.

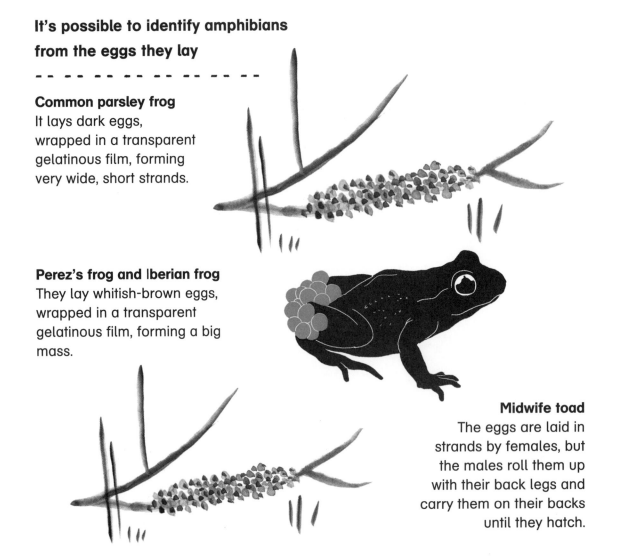

Midwife toad
The eggs are laid in strands by females, but the males roll them up with their back legs and carry them on their backs until they hatch.

The mystery of the disappearing frogs

A few years ago, scientists noticed that various species of amphibians were at the point of extinction all over the world. We don't know exactly what's causing this decline (which is the name for this type of large-scale extinction), but we think it could be several things happening at the same time:

- One of the reasons may be the destruction of habitats. Without places to live and find food, amphibians can't survive.
- Another reason may be the appearance of new predators (animals that eat amphibians and previously didn't exist in their habitats), a phenomenon that often happens because humans take species to places where they didn't exist before (called the introduction of exotic species). For example, the Louisiana crawfish (which comes from the United States) was introduced to rivers in Europe. This crawfish eats the larvae of many European species, and since the "European" amphibians aren't familiar with the crawfish, they don't flee and are easily caught.
- Other reasons include diseases caused by fungi and viruses, an increase in toxic substances in the environment, climate change, etc.

And why do amphibians suffer more from these problems than other animals in the wild?

Because their skin is very permeable, which means it lets substances through. When water gets polluted, it's easy for dangerous substances to pass through amphibians' skins and get into their bodies. The same thing happens with toxins or fungi that are in the air or on the soil. Biologists discovered all this when studying animals at risk of extinction. One of the first species they investigated was the golden toad (*Incilius periglenes*), which lived in Costa Rica and is now extinct.

Frog or toad?

It is not so easy to tell the difference between frogs and toads at first sight. Normally people call frogs the animals with smoother skin that live close to water, and they call toads the ones with rougher skin that spend more time on land. But in fact, frogs and toads are related, and scientists don't think there's any real difference between them.

Tree frogs are easier to identify because they have a kind of suckers on their feet, which makes them such good climbers.

Some unique species

The **Iberian spadefoot toad** got its name because it has a kind of black spade (a callus) on its back legs. It helps it bury itself in sand to escape from predators and to hide from the sun and survive in the dry season.

The **fire salamander** got its name because people say it hatches in the flames of fire. This story must have come about because these animals sometimes hide in firewood and so when people were about to light the fire, salamanders would start to come out. After all, no one likes to be roasted— not even a salamander!

toad

tree frog

Would you like to kiss a frog
to see what happens? You
shouldn't! Instead of bringing
you a prince, kissing one will
probably just make you itch.

Victors and victims

We know of almost 7,400 species of amphibians across the whole world. Some have adapted themselves to very particular habitats and even a small change could be enough to make them extinct. There are other species that aren't so specialized, which means they're able to live in very different habitats, distributing themselves in various countries or even whole continents. And when one of these more adaptable species is taken by humans to another region, the consequences are almost always bad.

A common amphibian victor
African clawed frog

The African clawed frog is a good example of a species that went far beyond its original area of distribution. It is native to the rivers and lakes of southeast Africa, but today the species is found throughout various parts of Europe, North America, South America, and Asia.

How did it all begin? The African clawed frog has often been chosen by scientists for laboratory experiments, such as the pregnancy test. In the past, women had to go to the doctor to find out if they were pregnant. A bit of their urine would be injected into a frog and if the woman was pregnant, the next morning there would be eggs in the aquarium! (Who knows how they discovered this!) It is thought that a lot of these animals were released into the wild when pregnancy tests stopped being done in this way. And that was when everything got messy.

These frogs are voracious and eat almost everything they come across—including the tadpoles of other amphibians. They also spread disease, and hence upset the balance of ecosystems around the world.

Some species that are victims

<u>Red-backed salamander</u>

While some amphibians have spread like a plague, others are suffering the consequences of the arrival of new species in their habitats. The Quito stubfoot toad and the Las Vegas Leopard frog are examples of amphibians that became extinct as a result of exotic species. The trout was responsible for the Quito stubfoot toad's disappearance, and in the case of the Las Vegas Leopard frog it was the bullfrog's fault. Even very abundant species can suffer the consequences of the introduction of exotics. This is the case of the red-backed salamander, a common species in various North American states. This long, thin salamander lives on land and likes hiding under tree trunks, moss and fallen leaves, in various kinds of forest. When there began to be exotic worms in some areas of the United States, it was verified that the number of salamanders decreased a lot. The worms reduce the amount of dead leaves on the forest floor, lowering the number of small animals that like this habitat and provide food for red-backed salamanders.

The salamander's trick

- - - - - - - - - -

The red-backed salamander is also an endangered species, and it has a unique ability: unlike most other amphibians, it can shed its tail to distract predators. While the predator is busy eating its tail, the salamander can run away! This ability to voluntarily cast off a body part, and still live, is called **autotomy**.

- - - - - - - - - -

They live in all regions of the planet, the North Pole and the South Pole, mountains and plains, deserts and big cities. They conquered the earth, the sky, and even the waves of the sea . . . They're birds, of course! When we see them gliding high above, we can't help but think . . .

I wish I could fly, too!

What distinguishes birds from other animals?

The thing that makes birds different from other animals is that their bodies are covered with feathers. Nowadays, this is the one characteristic that only birds have. But this wasn't always the case. Millions of years ago, there were other animals with feathers that today we would not necessarily consider birds—certain dinosaurs. Because of this, some scientists believe that birds should belong to the reptiles group.

Who's right?

We don't know, but one thing is certain: birds descended from dinosaurs, specifically from the same group of dinosaurs as the famous *Tyrannosaurus rex*. Scientists have even discovered some similarities between this fearsome predator and . . . the chicken!

The truth is that birds and reptiles today are so different that most scientists put them in different groups.

If it flies is it a bird?

No. There are lots of animals that fly but aren't birds: lots of insects, such as flies and butterflies, and even some mammals, such as bats. But no one flies as many hours straight and as far as some birds, not even most airplanes.

Which bird holds the world record?

One record holder is, without doubt, the bar-tailed godwit, which is able to fly almost 7,500 mi (12,000 km) without stopping (from Alaska to New Zealand). Bar-tailed godwits take about nine days to complete this journey, during which they don't eat or drink.

How can birds fly like that?

Birds manage this feat because their bodies are well adapted for flying.

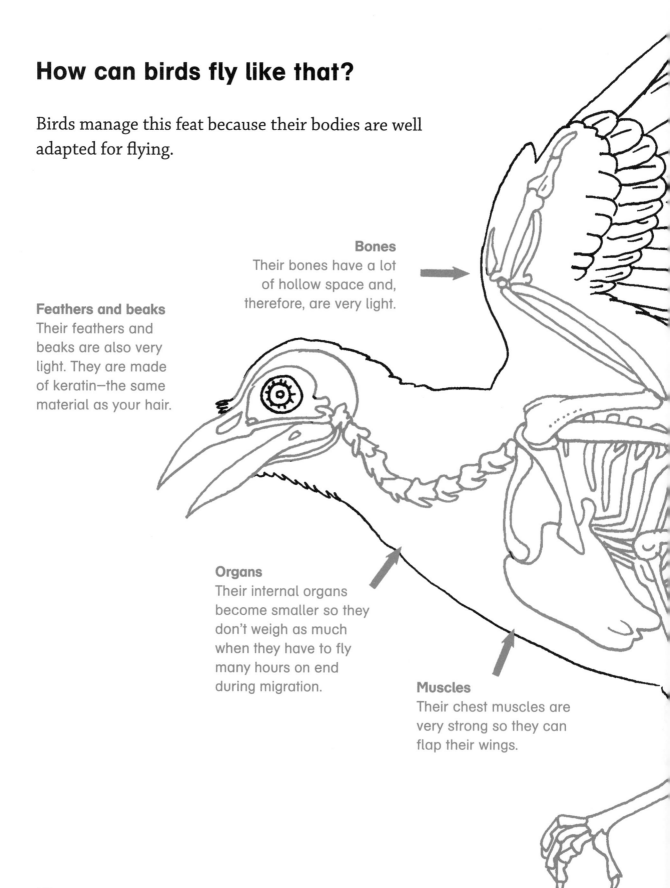

Bones
Their bones have a lot of hollow space and, therefore, are very light.

Feathers and beaks
Their feathers and beaks are also very light. They are made of keratin—the same material as your hair.

Organs
Their internal organs become smaller so they don't weigh as much when they have to fly many hours on end during migration.

Muscles
Their chest muscles are very strong so they can flap their wings.

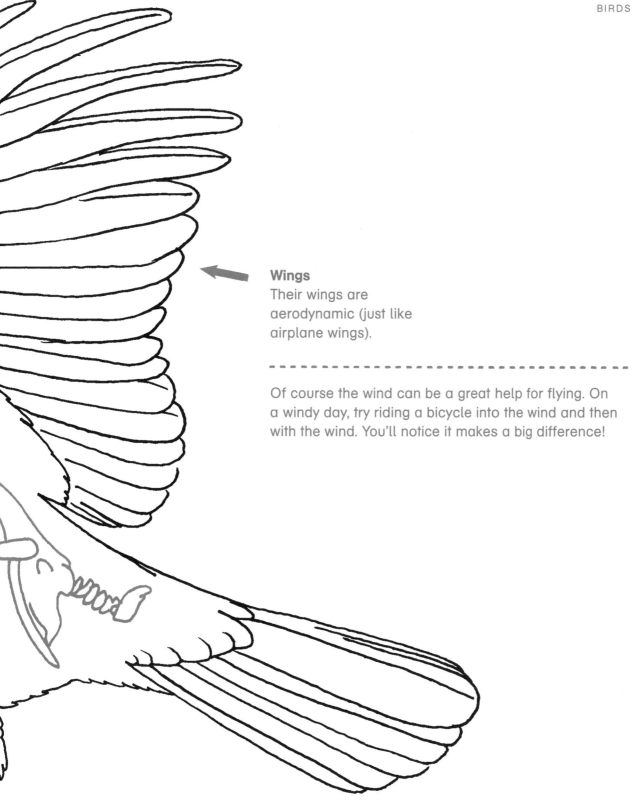

Wings
Their wings are
aerodynamic (just like
airplane wings).

- -

Of course the wind can be a great help for flying. On
a windy day, try riding a bicycle into the wind and then
with the wind. You'll notice it makes a big difference!

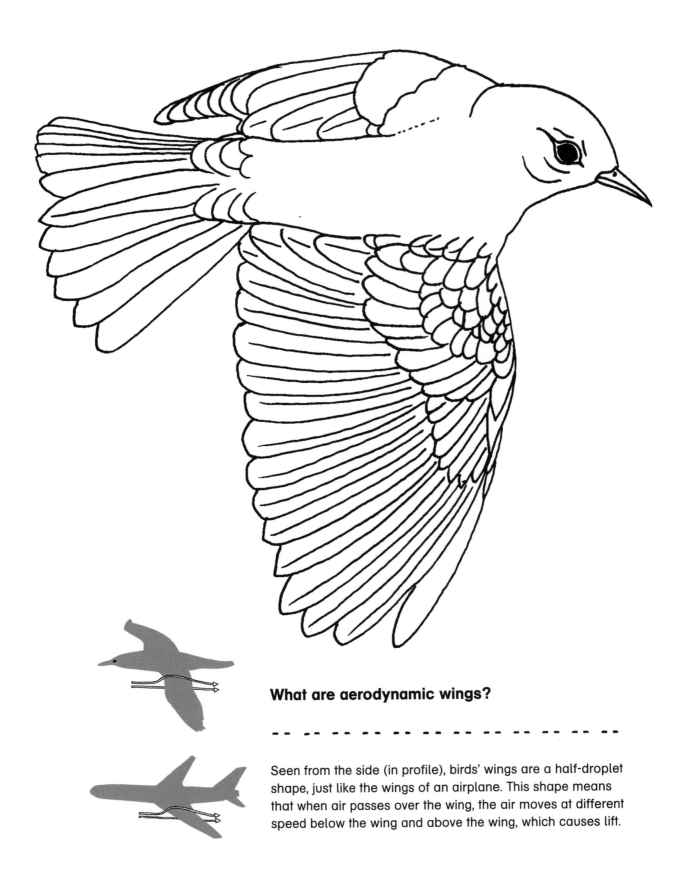

What are aerodynamic wings?

Seen from the side (in profile), birds' wings are a half-droplet shape, just like the wings of an airplane. This shape means that when air passes over the wing, the air moves at different speed below the wing and above the wing, which causes lift.

Which is the fastest bird?

The peregrine falcon. When it's hunting in a nosedive, it can fly at over 180 mph (300 kph)! In fact, the peregrine falcon isn't just the fastest bird—it's the fastest animal there is.

- -

And which bird flies the highest?

The species of bird that tends to fly highest is the bar-headed goose. This goose lives in Asia, and during its annual migration, it crosses the Himalayas (the highest mountains in the world).
Scientists put small GPS units on their backs and proved that these geese can fly at an altitude of 23,000 ft (7 km)!

But watch out . . .
The bird that was found flying at the highest altitude was not a goose: it was a Rüppell's vulture, which was flying at 36,000 ft (11 km) and crashed into an airplane flying at the same altitude. The bird died, but the airplane was able to land safely, even though it was damaged.

- -

And which bird flaps its wings the most?

This is, unquestionably, the amethyst woodstar hummingbird. All hummingbirds flap their wings very fast, but this one is able to flap its wings 80 times per second. And all to stay still in front of flowers while it drinks their nectar.

And which bird migrates the farthest?

One of the birds that fly the farthest without stopping is, as you already know, the bar-tailed godwit. But the one that migrates farthest of all is the Arctic tern, which, every fall, flies from the Arctic Sea to the Antarctic. After five years, an Arctic tern will have flown as many miles as the distance between the earth and the moon! This species also holds the record in another category: it is the animal that spends the most time in summer—it's as though it's constantly chasing summer and the mildest temperatures.

- - - - - - - - - -

If chickens are birds, why don't they fly?

Actually, chickens are able to flutter a bit, and their cousins that live in the wild in Southeast Asia are able to fly for real. But there are some birds that can't even flutter because their ancestors stopped needing to fly and they lost that ability. The most well-known of these are ostriches and penguins.

Where do penguins live?

Penguins live only in the cold waters of the most southerly oceans. But in other regions, there are birds with similar characteristics, even though they're not related to penguins, such as the guillemot and razorbill. These birds haven't lost their ability to fly, but they do dive very deep in the sea like penguins do, and, just like penguins, they look like they're wearing a black tuxedo with a white shirt. Why do you think that is?

When they're in the water with their bellies down, razorbills are difficult for the fish below them to see because their white bellies are easily confused with the surface of the sea, where the light comes from. Meanwhile, they're also difficult to see for the animals that are above them because their black backs are easily confused with the dark depths of the sea. This way they go unnoticed by their prey (when they're hunting) and by their predators (when they try to catch them).

airo

How can there be birds everywhere?

No other animal group is as well distributed around the world as birds. And the key to this success is, once again, their ability to fly.

By flying, birds are able to reach remote areas that few animals can get to. Also, their bodies have adapted to the characteristics of different habitats, and this is why they're different sizes and colors and have different beaks and feet.

Different kinds of feet

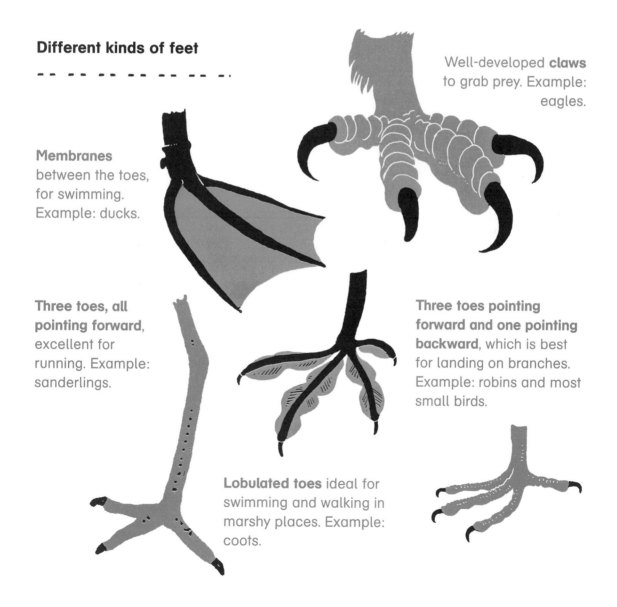

Membranes between the toes, for swimming. Example: ducks.

Well-developed **claws** to grab prey. Example: eagles.

Three toes, all pointing forward, excellent for running. Example: sanderlings.

Three toes pointing forward and one pointing backward, which is best for landing on branches. Example: robins and most small birds.

Lobulated toes ideal for swimming and walking in marshy places. Example: coots.

Different kinds of beaks

-- -- -- -- -- -- -- -

Birds' beaks are adapted to the different kind of things they eat. Some beaks are better for eating seeds, others for catching fish.

Shearwater

Just like the beaks of other marine birds, the shearwater's beak is very well adapted to life at sea. It uses it to catch the fish and squid it eats and, through the small tubes on the upper part, it gets rid of the excess salt from its food.

Hawfinch

The hawfinch has one of the strongest beaks adapted for eating seeds. It is so strong that it can break open a cherry pit!

Woodpecker

The woodpecker has a very strong beak, which it uses to make holes in tree trunks. It then pushes its long, sticky tongue into the holes and is able to pull out insects to eat.

Nightjar

This nocturnal bird eats insects that it catches while flying. To help it do this, it has long, very sensitive bristles around its mouth that help it detect prey in the darkness.

Arctic tern

This bird eats small fish, which it catches by diving from the air. Its narrow beak is adapted for this kind of hunting.

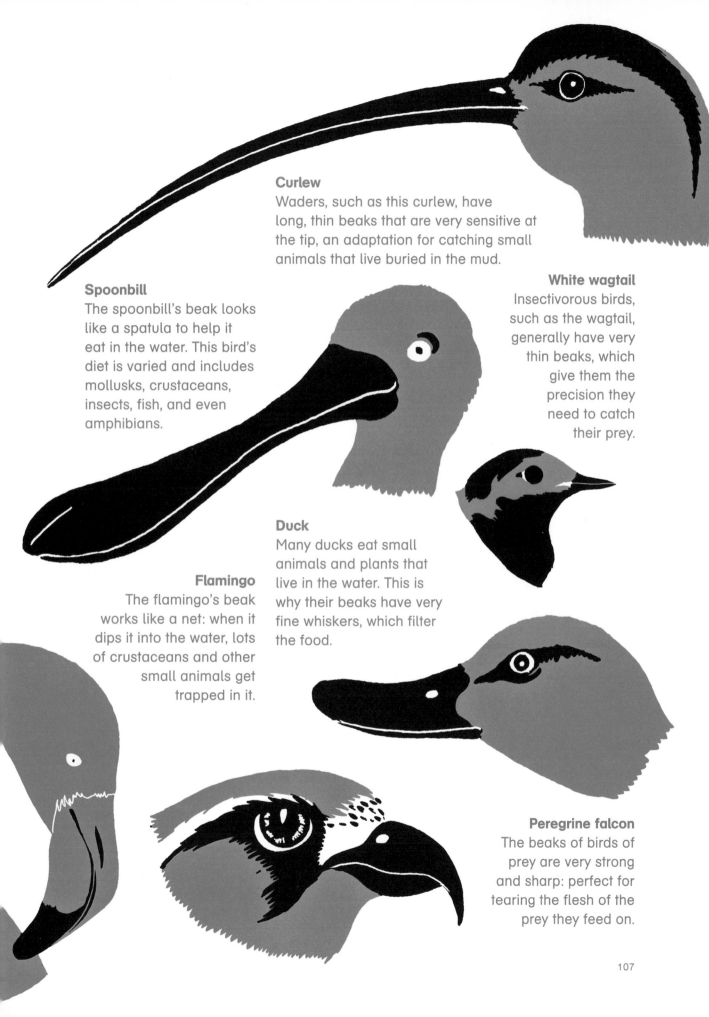

Curlew
Waders, such as this curlew, have long, thin beaks that are very sensitive at the tip, an adaptation for catching small animals that live buried in the mud.

Spoonbill
The spoonbill's beak looks like a spatula to help it eat in the water. This bird's diet is varied and includes mollusks, crustaceans, insects, fish, and even amphibians.

White wagtail
Insectivorous birds, such as the wagtail, generally have very thin beaks, which give them the precision they need to catch their prey.

Duck
Many ducks eat small animals and plants that live in the water. This is why their beaks have very fine whiskers, which filter the food.

Flamingo
The flamingo's beak works like a net: when it dips it into the water, lots of crustaceans and other small animals get trapped in it.

Peregrine falcon
The beaks of birds of prey are very strong and sharp: perfect for tearing the flesh of the prey they feed on.

Where do they choose to make their nests?

Birds are very careful about the places they choose to build their nests. After all, that's where they're going to lay their eggs and where their baby chicks will hatch! Whether it's on the ground, in a tree, in a cave, or in a hole in a garage wall, the most important thing is that the nest is safe from predators.

Types and locations of nests

There are species that make their nests on the ground and surround them with small stones so they're better disguised and protected.

Some make their nests in small caves . . .

. . . others use holes in trees.

Many small birds make nests among the leaves of plants or in the branches of trees. (These nests are normally cup-shaped.)

Some birds take advantage of human structures (for example, utility poles and roofs) to make their nests. This is the case with swallows and storks.

Many species of vulture choose to nest on ledges close to rivers.

How do I put up a birdhouse?

- -

Some important tips:

- Birds are more likely to move into your birdhouse if you put it in an area with few trees and, most important, few old trees (which are the ones that have the most holes and recesses).

- The best time to put up your birdhouse is at the end of autumn or the beginning of winter. This is because around the middle of winter, birds start looking for holes to make their nests, and if they find an empty birdhouse, they might choose it!

- Put your birdhouse in a place protected by branches so that it isn't very exposed, for example, on a branch that's partially covered by vegetation, and protected from the sun. Be careful, too, that the entrance is facing away from prevailing winds. This way, the birds will be better protected from cold, wind, and rain.

- Put the box at least 10–13 ft (3–4 m) off the ground and facing slightly downward so that rain can't get in so easily and build up inside.

- Remember that your birdhouse might not be occupied the first spring after you put it up. This can take a while or might never happen: don't forget that it's more likely to be successful when there are fewer old trees nearby.

NOTE: In some cases, it can be useful to put a bit of sand or vegetation inside your birdhouse. If it ends up being occupied, for example, by little owls, which don't make a nest, this will be useful to stop their eggs from rolling around.

blackcap

Why do birds sing?

Have you heard a robin sing on a spring morning? Or a blackcap? Birds are famous for their singing. In most species, it's the males that do the most singing. They use their song to attract females, but also to warn other males not to come too close: "Hey, don't come over here—this territory is mine!"

Record the sounds of birds

Choose a place where there are lots of birds and make a recording of the sounds they make. Later on, you can try to identify them from their songs, or you can simply enjoy listening to the recording.

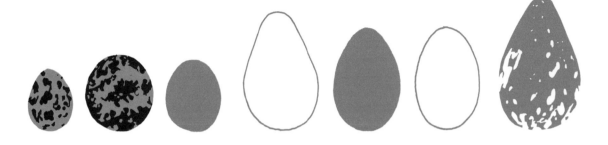

Do all birds lay eggs?

Yes, all birds lay eggs, but eggs from different birds can vary quite a bit. There are big and small eggs, rounder or longer eggs, dark and light, spotted, rough, or smooth. All of them start off having a yolk and a white inside, which, as the days go by, may turn into a chick.

How old are chicks when they leave the nest?

Some chicks hatch in a hurry and full of energy—just a few minutes after they leave the egg, they start running and are already able to eat on their own (partridges, for example). Other chicks stay in the nest for weeks (sometimes months!), being fed by their parents, which rush around trying to find food to bring them, like blackbird chicks, which stay in the nest for between two and three weeks.

Different kinds of eggs

- - -- -- -- -- -- -

It's often enough to see the color and shape of eggshells to identify which bird they belong to. You have to know which species nest in the area where the eggs were found, and compare them with the pictures in a specialized guide.

What do birds eat?

The answer seems obvious: birdseed, of course! But only some birds (especially the ones in cages) eat this. The ones that live in the wild, the ones we see outside, eat quite a variety of things. Biologists group birds according to what they eat, but this isn't always an easy job. Some birds like to confuse us and eat different kinds of food according to what they like or what is available. Here are some examples of how they are generally divided:

Granivorous and frugivorous birds (the "vegetarians") eat mainly seeds and fruit. Example: sparrows.

Piscivorous birds eat mainly fish. Examples: kingfishers and ospreys.

Insectivorous birds eat insects, spiders, or worms. Examples: flycatchers and bee-eaters.

sparrow

flycatcher

bee-eater

osprey

kingfisher

peregrine falcon

The peregrine falcon: a success story

Peregrine falcons exist almost all over the world, and can be seen both in the country and in urban areas—they sometimes even makes nests in buildings in big cities. But it wasn't always this way. In the middle of the last century, the peregrine falcon was a species in danger of extinction.

The main causes of their decline were direct hunting or poisoning by use of pesticides in agriculture, such as DDT. But scientists discovered what was happening in time, and thanks to conservation efforts we can still admire this species, which is among the most amazing predators of the animal kingdom.

As you already know, the peregrine falcon is the fastest animal that exists. There's only one reason it flies so fast: it feeds almost exclusively on other birds, which it catches mid-flight. This is why it has to be faster than its prey.

Peregrine falcons are also well known for the incredible migrations they make: some fly up to 9,300 mi (15,000 km) every year, between the places where they reproduce and spend the winter. When they're traveling, they can cover up to 118 mi (190 km) in a single day.

Other facts about peregrine falcons:

- They're very faithful birds: when they choose a mate or territory, it's for life.
- They can be found in a variety of habitats—deserts, tundras, tropical zones, and cities.
- Females lay between three and four eggs, which are incubated by both males and females.

How do I identify species of birds?

You will need:
A pair of binoculars
A field guide to identifying birds
A notebook
Colored pencils

- Start in the nearest yard or garden. On a sunny morning, nice and early, go out and observe the birds that fly by and also those that land on the ground, a post, a shrub, or a branch.

- If you have binoculars, you'll be able to see some details. Notice the size of the bird, its coloring, the size and shape of its beak and feet, and its behavior: is it singing? Is it looking for something? Is it standing still or hopping around?

- Notice, too, if it's alone or in a group with other birds.

- Try to hear the song: How would you characterize it? High pitched? Deep? Continuous? Does it have breaks? What does the song sound like?

- Then look in your field guide for the birds you saw. Some species are very similar, and at first, it might seem difficult to distinguish them. But with experience, you'll see that it gets easier and easier.

Why are there only swallows in spring?

Just as we sometimes take summer vacations far away from home, there are many species of birds that decide to make a long journey to a faraway place once a year. But birds make this journey in order to survive: some because they can't bear the cold; others because there's no more food in the places they live (perhaps due to snow); other birds journey for both of these reasons. This journey is called migration.

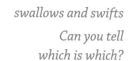

Where do birds migrate to?
Some migrate nearby, but others can migrate to the other side of the planet.

swallows and swifts
Can you tell
which is which?

Are there migrant birds outside?
Yes, there are. Depending on where do you live, and on the season, so you can find different species. For example, ducks and waders usually breed in Northern latitudes, such as the arctic and sub-arctic regions, and move to warmer places to spend the winter months. During this period you can find them in wetlands and coastal areas of most temperate regions. Many small birds prefer to spend the winter in the Southern hemisphere, and return to breed during spring. Some famous examples are the swifts, the swallows, and the cuckoos.

great spotted
cuckoo

Endangered species

Humans and birds have a long history, but birds don't always come out on top. Many species of birds are becoming extinct due to the destruction of their habitats, hunting, or illegal capture.

Vultures and bustards are two particularly endangered groups of birds.

Do you want to help save the birds from extinction?

- - - - - - - - - - - - - -

Around the world, there are more than 1,300 species of birds in danger of extinction. But fortunately, there are also lots of people concerned with guaranteeing their survival.

You can help, too, directly, by participating in conservation work, or indirectly, by talking to your friends and classmates about efforts to help these species.

If interested, contact a nature conservation organization. (See the list at the end of this book.)

- - - - - - - - - - - - - -

bustard

vulture

Are you interested in seeing a migration?

Even though birds don't stay very long during a migration (since they're only passing through), it's relatively easy to spot them.

Keep these tips in mind:

- August and November are the best months to see migratory birds, but April and May can also be good.

- During migration periods, there are migratory birds everywhere, but you'll see the biggest groups of birds at estuaries and lakes.

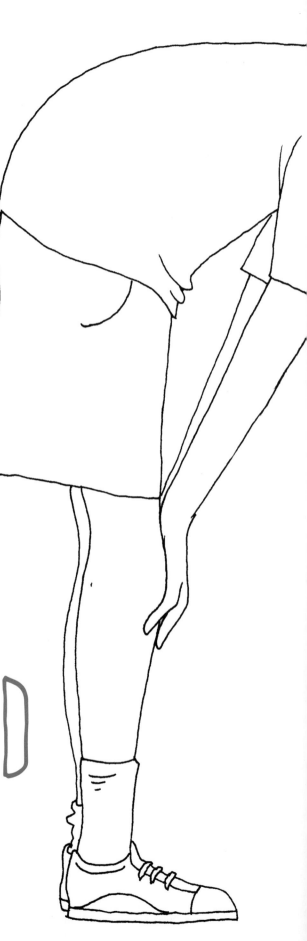

ALWAYS CLOSE TO THE GROUND

REPTILES

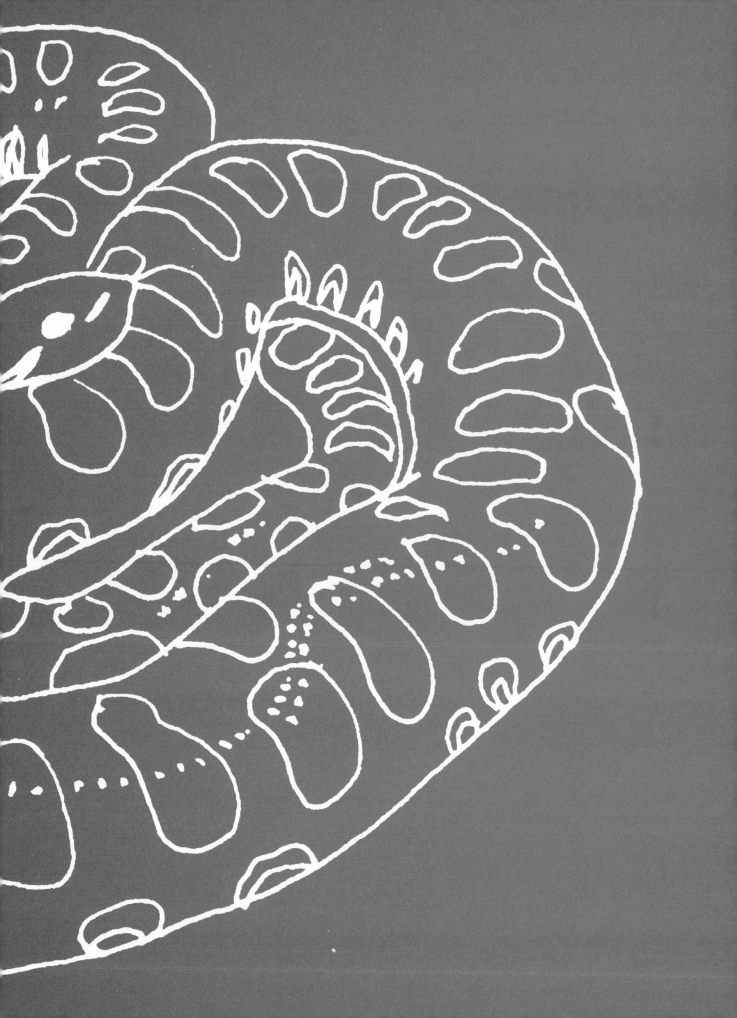

The word reptile comes from the Latin *reptile*, which means "one that creeps." Lots of people are frightened (maybe even terrified!) of this group of animals. But with the exception of some with poisonous venom, there's no real reason for us to be afraid of them.

Find them outside . . . always close to the ground (or perched on a wall).

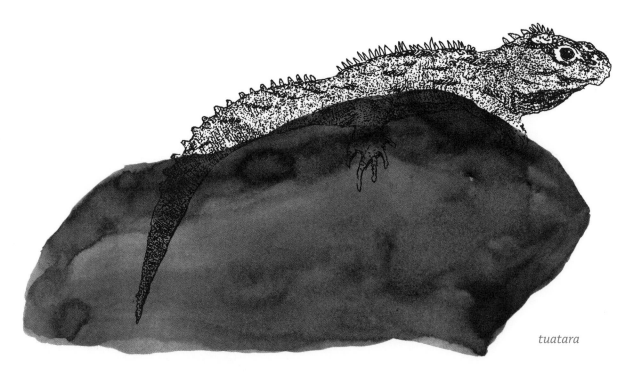

tuatara

What are reptiles?

We say these animals are cold-blooded, but if we touch them in the spring or summer, they can feel very warm. This is because reptiles are animals whose body temperature varies according to the temperature of their environment: their bodies don't produce their own heat (like our bodies do)—it comes from external conditions.

Before it eats breakfast, a reptile needs to warm up, or else it won't have enough energy to catch food. That's why we so often see lizards sitting in the sun! Biologists call these animals ectotherms.

Unlike amphibians, reptiles spend most of their time on land and not in the water. That's why their bodies need scales—so they don't dehydrate and lose too much water.

To sum up: a reptile is a cold-blooded animal with a body covered in scales, and it almost always creeps along the ground.

Show me your scales!

What are scales made from?

Reptiles' scales are made from keratin, which is also the material that our hair and nails, as well as birds' feathers and beaks, are made of.

Are reptile scales the same as fish scales?

No, they're slightly different: reptile scales are made from the most superficial, or outer-most, part of the skin (the epidermis), and fish scales are made from the deepest part of the skin (the dermis).

Are all scales the same?

Some reptiles, for example snakes, lizards, and geckos, have small scales, but turtles and tortoises have large scales called <u>scutes</u> (1).

Chameleons have scales that look like small bumps, called <u>granular</u> scales (2).

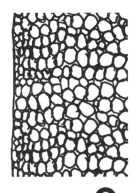

Adders and water snakes (*Natrix* spp.) have <u>keeled</u> scales (3), which are divided down the middle by a line that sticks up slightly. (This is one of the reasons why these two species are so often mistaken for each other.)

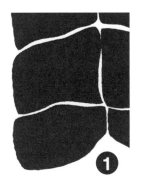

The large psammodromus, a kind of sand lizard, has <u>imbricate</u> scales (4), which overlap one another slightly like tiles on a roof.

What are they?

There are lots of different reptiles around the world. They are put into groups based on what they have in common. The tuatara, crocodile, and turtle and tortoise groups are the oldest. All the other reptiles are more recent, but they resemble one another and belong to a large group called Squamata.

Turtles and tortoises

This is the oldest group of reptiles in the world—it has existed since the time of the dinosaurs! It includes sea, land, and freshwater turtles. Examples: European pond turtles and red-eared sliders.

Worm lizards

Reptiles in this group look like big worms, but they have a spinal column and scales.

Tuataras

This group only has one genus of reptile: the tuatara, which only exists in New Zealand. It's another very old group. (Also, they have a special characteristic you'll learn about soon.)

Snakes and vipers

This group includes all snakes, poisonous or not. Examples: adders and kingsnakes.

Chameleons, geckos, lizards, slowworms, and western three-toed skinks

This group includes the most species. Examples: sand lizards and common chameleons.

Crocodiles

This group is made up of only crocodiles, which, just like turtles, have lived on our planet for millions of years.

Hylonomus lyelli

How long have they been around?

Reptiles have been around on Earth for more than 300 million years!

A reptile called *Hylonomus lyelli* is the oldest that has been found so far. (Scientists are always discovering new things, and tomorrow there could be a "new" oldest.)

From these first reptiles came all others, a process that took millions of years. Charles Darwin called this evolution. Many reptiles that evolved from this first group are already extinct, as is the case with dinosaurs, but there are others, such as tortoises, that are as old as the dinosaurs and still around!

●

Look at (real) dinosaur footsteps!

- -

Dinosaur tracks can be found in many places!

The longest continuous set of dinosaur footprints in the world can be found in Colorado along the Purgatoire River. The footprints were made in the late Jurassic period by dinosaurs that include Iguanodon, Apatosaurus, Coelurus, and Triceratops.

Some of the best-known dinosaur footprints on Earth are in Glen Rose, Texas,

by the banks of the Paluxy River. These tracks were made by large sauropods, two-legged carnivores, and some smaller two-legged herbivores. There are even some small footprints that look as though they could have been made by humans – but in fact they belong to small, bipedal dinosaurs.

In the UK, you can see fossilized footprints at low tide on Brook Beach, on the Isle of Wight.

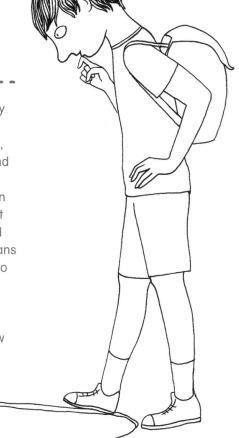

- -

Egyptian mongoose

What do they eat? And what eats them?

Most reptiles are carnivores, but some tortoises and large lizards, such as iguanas, are vegetarians or omnivores. Some snakes almost always eat eggs; others prefer to eat other reptiles.

But reptiles are also food for a lot of animals. This is the case with the short-toed snake eagle. Mongooses love eating snakes, too, and some snakes love eating chameleons. Even we humans eat reptiles: in some countries, people eat crocodile steak, turtle soup, stuffed snake, and lots of other delicacies.

Defense strategies (and some theater . . .)

Because they have a lot of predators, reptiles invented a sort of theatricality to defend themselves—biologists call this defense strategies. Depending on the danger, reptiles act out one of their favorite scenes:

- They inflate their bodies to seem larger than they actually are.
- They open their mouths wide and make threatening noises.

- They disguise themselves as whatever is around them, as chameleons do. This is called mimicry.
- They imitate more dangerous species. For example, the viperine snake holds its head so it looks like a viper and even attacks like a viper.
- They pretend to be dead. When they feel threatened, viperine snakes lie still and leave off a horrible smell.
- Lots of lizards and geckos drop their tail, which can keep moving on its own and look like an animal wriggling. When the predator goes to grab the tail, the lizard can take the opportunity to escape.
- If none of the other tricks work, they bite . . .

How many eyes do reptiles have?

Reptiles have two eyes plus an extra one: the pineal eye. This eye is found on the top of the head, right in the middle, but it isn't used for seeing anything: it just gives the animal an idea about the light that's around it. The reptiles with the most developed pineal eyes are the tuatara, which, as you know, are a very old species that live in New Zealand.

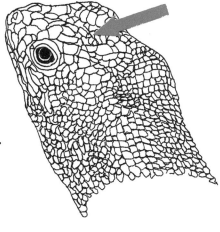

Speaking of crocodiles . . .

- - - - - - - - -

The world's largest reptile is the saltwater crocodile (*Crocodylus porosus*), which can grow up to 23 ft (7 m) long and weigh over 3,300 lb (1,500 kg).

And before the egg?

- - - - - - - - -

You need a male and a female to make an egg. Each one has its own kind of seed to make other reptiles. For the male, this is called a spermatozoid, and for the female, it is called an ovule. When the two come together, they form an egg. You might be thinking, *But that's how it always is!*

But is it? Actually no. There are always exceptions. And lizards are proof of this. In certain places, there are only female lizards, and they're able to make eggs using only their own ovules! The problem is that all the lizards come out identical to their mother and no males are ever born. This is called parthenogenesis.

How are baby reptiles born?

Almost all reptiles are <u>oviparous</u>, meaning their babies are born from eggs. The eggs are normally buried in the ground, and when the babies are born, they're ready to start their lives on their own.

Very rarely, like with some crocodiles, females make nests, lay the eggs, and stay to look after them until the babies are born (and even afterward, when the babies are still very small).

There are some reptiles, like vipers, that don't lay eggs: the babies grow inside the egg, inside the mother's belly, and the egg only comes out when the baby is born. (These animals are <u>ovoviviparous</u>.)

There are also species such as many skinks, which are <u>viviparous,</u> and produce living young.

Nasty as a snake!

People often portray reptiles as unpleasant: they say snakes are evil and poisonous, and that geckos are poisonous and their skin is sticky. There are even stories that people swear are true, but are nothing more than folktales. (You can read one of these stories on the left.)

Do reptiles deserve this reputation?

Of course not! Most reptiles aren't sticky or poisonous—there are exceptions, but these are rare. Their scaly skin is dry and not moist. In fact, snakeskin is very silky and even pleasant to the touch. (But never touch a snake in the wild if you see one!)

All living things have a function in their environment, and reptiles are no exception. Have you ever thought what would happen if reptiles disappeared? There could be a big increase in lots of other species, and this would cause an imbalance in nature. For example, geckos eat a lot of mosquitoes, and snakes eat a lot of rats: if there were no geckos or snakes, the number of mosquitoes and rats would go up tremendously!

For people who like scary stories . . .

- - - - - - - -

Some Europeans say they know somebody who died from drinking from a cup a gecko had fallen in. That's nonsense! Geckos aren't poisonous, and if they do fall off the roof (and land in a cup), it's just because they've been up there hunting insects . . .

Do you know what a herpetologist is?

It's a scientist who studies reptiles and amphibians. The word herpetologist comes from the Greek *herpeton*, which means "reptile." At first, herpetology was a science that studied only reptiles, but later it changed to include amphibians as well (the first group of vertebrates to live out of water).

Pretend you're a herpetologist

Go on an outing to the countryside to try to find some species. Bring a camera so you can take your time to identify what you find. (You can look at the pictures later.) Make a list of all the reptiles you see (on that day and on others).

Tips:
When to look?
The best time to look, without a doubt, is springtime, when it's sunny. In winter, it's very cold and these animals hibernate; in summer, they hide away during the hottest hours.

Where to look?
The best way to see them is when they come out to sunbathe. Look on walls, stones, tree trunks, or other objects in the sun.

Which are the easiest to see?
Lizards are the reptiles that are some of the most common and easiest to see.

Tricks:
- Try attracting a lizard with a little stick with honey or some fruit on it. Wait patiently and the lizard should come closer.

- Some reptiles, such as geckos, go out at night and sleep in the day, so to see them, you can look in the evening. In summer, geckos appear on the walls of houses, mainly underneath lights, waiting for insects.
- You can also look for geckos in the daytime, when they're resting in dark and peaceful places (e.g., mailboxes).

Shall we pop over to an island?

When an animal arrives on an island for the first time, everything is different: there might not be the same species as on the mainland, there might not even be predators that want to eat it—and this can obviously be an advantage. If nothing wants to hunt it, the animal leads a more relaxed, longer life and this change can mean that its behavior alters.

With time, if the animals on the mainland and those that moved to the island are separated for many years, different species may develop. Evolution at work once again!

For example, in Madagascar, which is an island on the east side of the African continent, there are over 300 species of reptiles and over 90% are endemic. Because Madagascar is a large island that has been isolated for millions of years, the reptiles that live there have been isolated from their relatives on the continent for all this time, which has given rise to different species.

The difference between native and endemic species

- - - - - - - - - - - -

Native species are species that naturally exist in a region or ecosystem. In other words, they exist without any-one having taken them there, but are not exclusive to that region (they can be native to other places).

Endemic species are native species that only exist in a given region of the planet, they don't naturally exist any-where else in the world.

How did animals get to islands, which are surrounded by water?

Some animals arrived during the Ice Age, when much more water was frozen, and the sea level was lower. And so some of the places that are islands today were originally linked to the mainland and were easier to reach!

Other animals—mainly those on islands a long way from the coast—were carried there on a boat (this often happened with mice and rats) or were taken there on purpose by humans. For example, humans have taken rabbits to islands. The rabbits reproduced very quickly and became an invasive species that had a big impact on the ecosystem.

There are even cases of animals that arrive on islands by flying, swimming, or using floating vegetation as a raft. In other words, all on their own, without human intervention.

Go to an island and see special lizards and geckos (and other animals, of course!)

- - - - - - - - - - - - - - - -

A planet with so much water, like ours, also has a lot of islands and islets. What about visiting one? Choose one close to your home (if you live near the sea) or take advantage of a vacation and persuade your parents to take you to one. It's best to choose one that's wilder so you can see more species (lots of islands are nature reserves). Don't forget to take comfortable shoes, a hat, a camera, and binoculars (to see the birds). Follow the tips in "Pretend you're a herpetologist". If there are no reptiles there, you can always pretend you're an ornithologist!

- - - - - - - - - - - - - - - -

wall lizard

Some brave it and take a dip in the ocean

Marine iguanas live on all the islands of the Galapagos archipelago. When Charles Darwin arrived at this archipelago and saw the marine iguanas for the first time he thought they were so ugly that he called them "disgusting clumsy lizards"! In fact, these reptiles do look a bit strange and they behave a bit strangely for a lizard, too: they're the only ones that eat in the ocean, eating seaweed.

Because they're ectothermic, their bodies cool down when they go to eat so they have to get back onto land to warm up in the sun. They're normally dark colored and this helps them absorb heat. (When you wear a black T-shirt and go out in the sun, doesn't it make you hotter?)

Other reptiles that like salt water

There are other reptiles that live in the ocean and never get out. This is the case with sea snakes, like the yellow-bellied sea snake.

Others, like sea turtles, live in the sea and only set foot on land to lay their eggs. This the case with the leatherback sea turtle. The females choose a beach in the area where they were born and lay their eggs—normally more than a hundred of them! Meanwhile, once the males have hatched and entered the water, they never get back on land again.

These leatherbacks are the biggest turtles that exist on Earth—they can grown up to 7 ft (2 m) long, and can weigh more than 1,500 lb (700 kg)! They mainly feed off jellyfish, and while they breathe air and come to the surface to take in oxygen, they can hold their breath and remain underwather for up to 85 minutes.

leatherback sea turtle

Chameleons

Chameleons are reptiles with very peculiar characteristics, which make them look strange and funny at the same time. Although they can vary in size, from 1 in (3 cm), up to 25 in (63 cm), they have a lot in common.

Most chameleons—especially the bigger species—have a long prehensile tail, which grabs things as if it was another hand; protruding eyes that can move in different directions at the same time; and a long tongue with a sticky tip. If a chameleon sees an insect, it stares at it, slowly gets ready, and fires its tongue. As soon as the tongue touches the insect, it sticks to it and moves back into the chameleon's mouth (but all this happens so fast that it's hard to see with the naked eye).

What is it that everyone knows about chameleons?
That they change color, of course! But why?

There are various reasons why chameleons change colour:
- To disguise themselves: chameleons's patterns make it more difficult for predators to find them in vegetation, so they're better protected.
- To thermoregulate (change their body temperature): when their bodies are cold, chameleons can turn darker, and because dark colors absorb more light, this makes them heat up more quickly when they're in the sun. The craziest thing is when chameleons are able to turn one side of their bodies dark and the other light!
- To "dress" according to their mood: the colors and patterns also depend on a chameleon's mood and are used to communicate. For example, when a female is pregnant she has a different pattern to warn males that she doesn't want to be with them anymore.

Courting chameleons

It's true chamleons like courting, but they also like to change partners—in other words, both males and females can mate with more than one partner. Some males even walk miles in search of a new female! The female chooses whether or not to accept him, if she thinks that he's more colorful or has showier horns than her other partner.

Eggs grow inside female chameleons's bellies for three to six weeks: at the end of this time they're ready to be born! Some chameleons are born directly from their mothers's bellies (viviparous), but most species are oviparous. In this case, the mothers look for a good place to bury their eggs. They dig a deep hole—and because the mothers have little feet, this job can take more than a day! After the hole is finished, they lay the eggs and cover everything carefully. This is such a big effort that it's common for them to die shortly afterward. The eggs stay buried for several months until the baby chameleons start to climb out. They all come out at the same time, and dig up to the surface and quickly try to find a tree to climb. Then their big adventure begins!

WHAT MAKES

US ALIKE?

MAMMALS

When we think of mammals, we might first think of an enormous lion or tiger! But big, hairy animals aren't the only ones in this group. Mammals can be enormous or very tiny, really hairy, almost bald, or even spiky. They can have legs, fins, or wings. They can swim in water, walk on land, or fly through the air . . . (And don't forget: humans are also mammals!)

So how are we all alike?

Where do we come from?

Mammals can be so different from one another that it's hard to believe they belong to the same group. But millions of years ago, there was an ancestor common to all of us . . .

What was this ancestor?

That ancestor belonged to a group called *Cynodontia*, which includes animals similar to reptiles and from which various species emerged. Some of these species are already extinct, but others evolved into other mammals that are alive today. In 2013, scientists made a model of this animal, common to all placental mammals. Although they can't be sure, they think this animal looked a bit like a shrew and ate insects. The oldest mammal fossils that have been found are of this species, but the case isn't closed just yet.

What happened next?

In a world full of very diverse environments—oceans, tropical forests, deserts, and frozen tundras—mammals have adapted so they can live in almost all of these places. Over millions of years, they acquired wings for flying, changed arms into fins for swimming, or grew lots of hair for protecting themselves from the cold—and these are only a few examples. Think of how different mammals are from one another!

Some mammals went *splash!*

Perhaps because there were already a lot of animals on land and there wasn't much to eat, some species started to use the oceans to find food. As time went by, they spent more and more time there and constantly adapted to life in the water. Over the course of millions of years, their arms turned into fins, their legs became a tail similar to a fish's, and their bodies took on a shape that made it easier to move through the water. This is how there came to be whales, dolphins, and seals, which are all aquatic mammals very well adapted to life in the water.

Do whales have noses?

Like all mammals, marine mammals breathe using lungs. (They have to come to the surface of the water to breathe.) Whales don't breathe through noses, but they do have a sort of nostril: a blowhole, which is on the top of their head. Whales breathe through there, and it's where that famous spurt of water comes out . . .

Do you know which animal has the biggest brain in the world?

The sperm whale! Its brain can weigh up to 20 lb (9 kg).

It's also the largest known mammal with teeth, the largest carnivore, the noisiest animal (it spurts water out of its blowhole up to over 30 ft [10 m] high!), and the best diver (it dives to over 6,500 ft [2,000 m])!

The sperm whale is the king of records!

Some mammals still prefer land

(but they decided to dig!)

Many mammals live on land, and there are some that even live underneath it! Moles, for example, dig long tunnels that lead to their burrows, where they sleep and have their babies. To dig the tunnels, they push the soil out and up to the surface, forming mounds, like the ones you can see in the country or in gardens.

Do you know how moles keep their food fresh?
Moles love eating worms. So that they always have worms available, moles bury worms in their burrows and bite the worms so they're paralyzed. This way the worms are alive but can't escape!

The Pyrenean desman: an endangered species
There is a kind of mole that lives in water instead of under the ground: the Pyrenean desman, which is very rare (only existing in certain parts of Portugal and Spain) and in danger of extinction. This mole lives in rivers where the water is clean and has small waves. It's very sensitive: if the river where it lives gets polluted or altered somehow (for example, by a dam), the Pyrenean desman will have to leave and find a new home.

Is it a ball of fur or a mole?

Pyrenean desmans are not easy to find because they leave their burrows only at night (the best time to hunt in the water).

The Pyrenean desman measures about 8 in (20 cm) in length and looks like a ball of fur.

Its fur is waterproof and keeps it warm. When the mole swims underwater, its fur gets a kind of metallic shine.

It has a trumpet-shaped snout, which never stops moving!

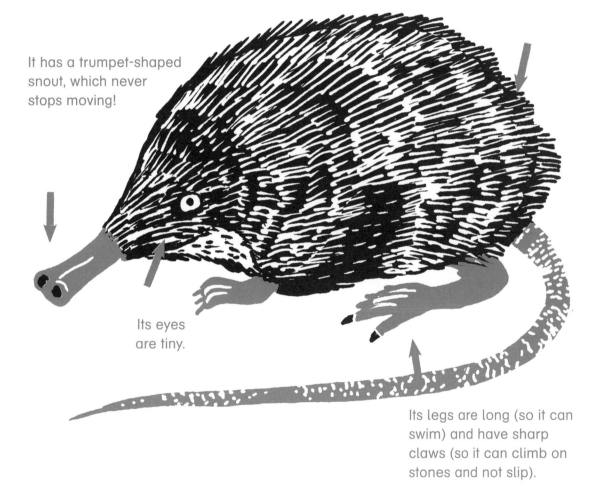

Its eyes are tiny.

Its legs are long (so it can swim) and have sharp claws (so it can climb on stones and not slip).

During the day, it can eat half its body weight in insects and other critters. That's a lot of food!

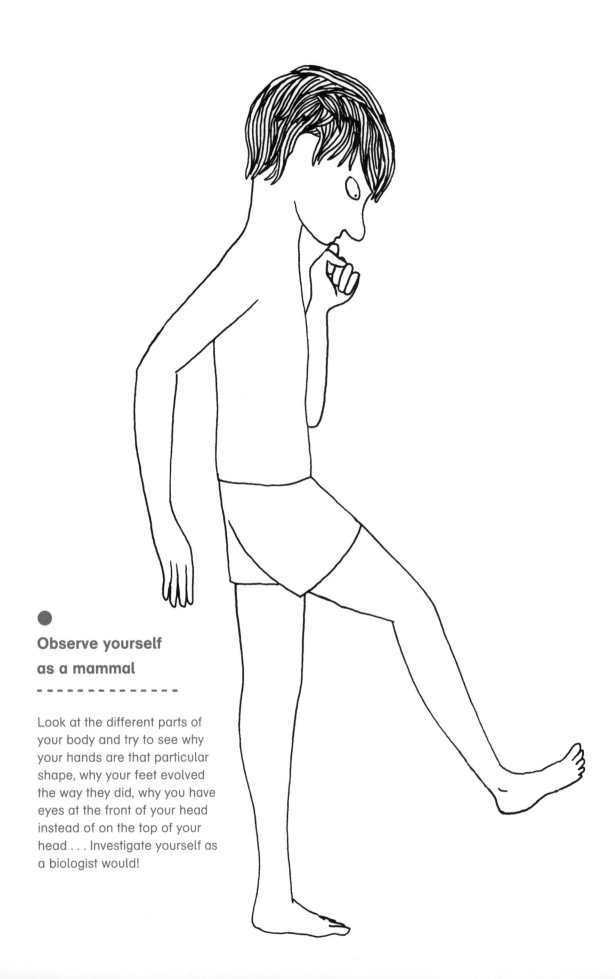

Observe yourself
as a mammal

- - - - - - - - - - - - - - -

Look at the different parts of
your body and try to see why
your hands are that particular
shape, why your feet evolved
the way they did, why you have
eyes at the front of your head
instead of on the top of your
head . . . Investigate yourself as
a biologist would!

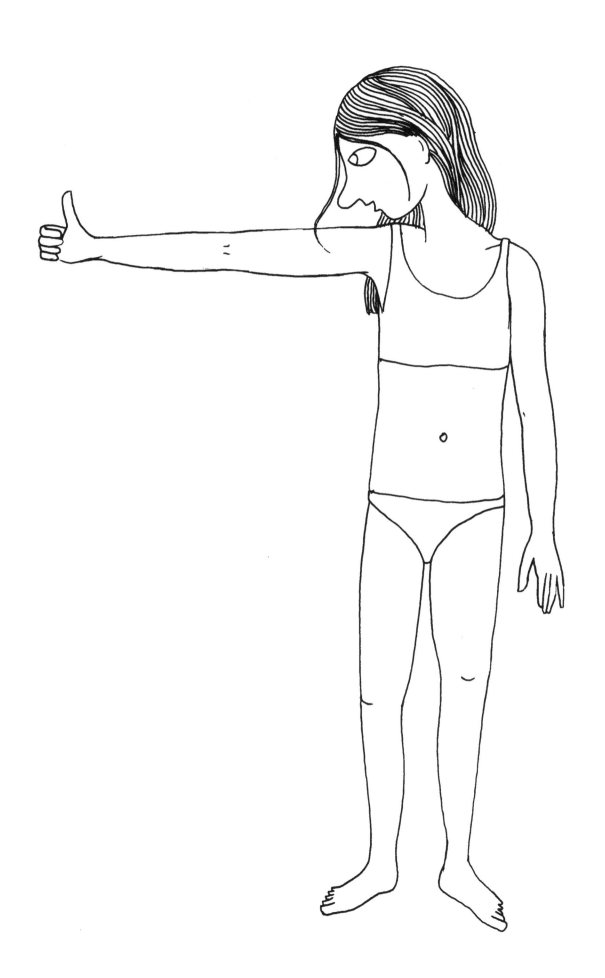

Mammals that fly above us

There are terrestrial mammals that hardly ever walk on land and instead spend a lot of time flying: bats!

Are there bats where I live?

It's quite possible! At night, especially on warm nights, you can see bats flying around streetlights in many towns and cities. Maybe you've already seen one but didn't realize it was a bat—they can be very small and very fast!

Have you noticed how bats' wings are similar to our arms?
Just like us, they have upper arms, forearms, and hands.

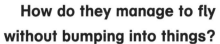

How do they manage to fly without bumping into things?

Even though bats have eyes and can see well, they also use their ears to find their way and avoid obstacles when they're flying. Bats make various sounds that we can't hear. These sounds move through the air as a wave, and when these waves meet an object, they bounce back. When these sound waves return to the bat, their ears transmit this information to their brain, which can then sense everything in front of it. This is called echolocation.

<u>Note:</u> There are bats (flying foxes) that only use their eyesight.

Why do bats sleep hanging from their feet?

Bats' ancestors were animals similar to shrews that walked on four legs. As these animals evolved, their front legs turned into wings and the knees on their back legs changed so they bent backward. Because of this, their legs are rather weak, so bats aren't able to stand on them (unlike birds, for example, which have stronger legs). Also, if they're hanging, bats are able to fly off more quickly.

So why don't bats fall when they're sleeping?

When we hang from the branch of a tree, we have to hold on tight with our hands. When we relax our muscles, our hands open and we fall to the ground. With bats, it's the other way around: when their muscles are relaxed, their feet close; and when they want to open their feet, bats have to make an effort to do so. That explains why their feet will never open when they're relaxed and sleeping!

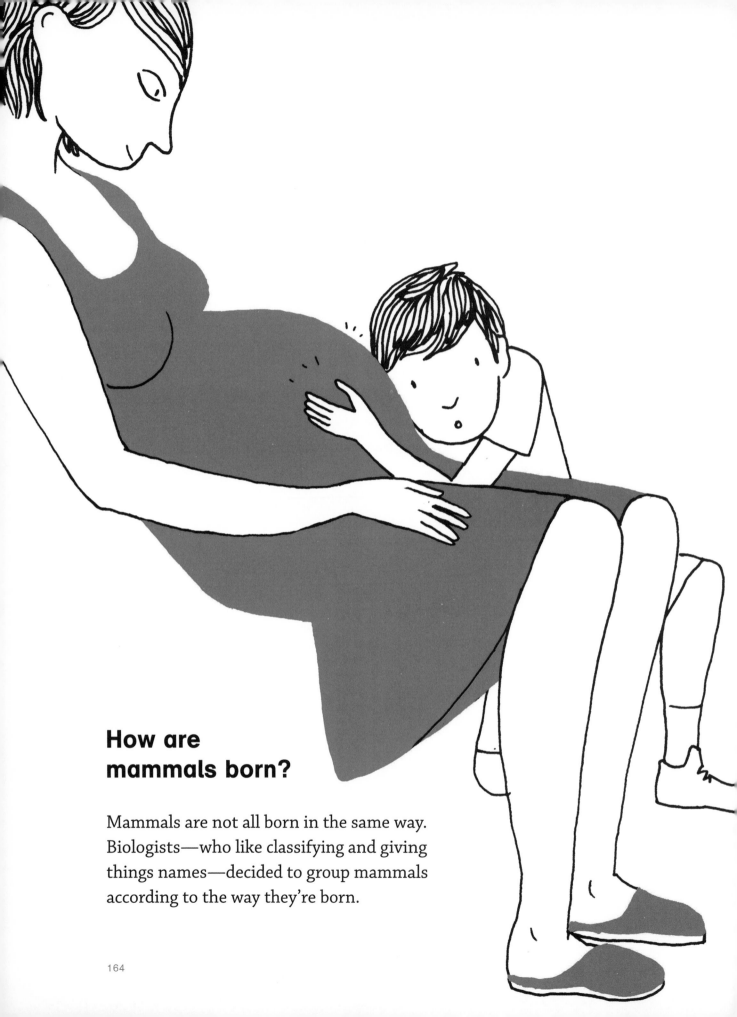

How are mammals born?

Mammals are not all born in the same way. Biologists—who like classifying and giving things names—decided to group mammals according to the way they're born.

Placental mammals

These mammals grow inside their mothers' bellies, where they're fed through an umbilical cord until they're developed enough to live outside of their mother. Most of the mammals we know of belong to this group. Examples: dogs, rats, bats, dolphins, tigers, hippopotamuses, wolves—and humans, of course!

Monotreme mammals

These mammals lay eggs that their babies hatch from, and just like all other mammals, the babies drink their mother's milk! This is the group with fewest species, and they exist only in Australasia. Examples: echidnas and platypuses.

Marsupial mammals

The females have a kind of pouch outside their bellies, called a marsupium. The babies are born very small, and with their eyes still closed, they climb into the marsupium. The mother's teats, full of milk, are in there, and the babies feed and grow. These animals mainly exist in Australasia and South America. Examples: koalas and kangaroos.

- -

What am I?

I have the beak and feet of a duck,
  but I'm not a duck.
I have the body of an otter,
  but I'm not an otter.
I have poison, but I'm not a snake.

Read on to find out the answer . . .

The **platypus**! This animal is so strange that the first time a stuffed specimen was brought from Australia to Europe, biologists thought that it was a hoax and that someone had stuck together parts of different animals! As well as having feet and a beak like a duck and a body like an otter, a platypus lays eggs. The male has a poisonous spur on each hind leg.

Have fun mixing animals

- - - - - - - - - - - - -

Take inspiration from the platypus and invent funny animals, mixing parts of different animals. Then you can make up names for your creations.

Do all mammals have fur?

Yes, but we can't always see it. Some only have fur when they're inside their mothers' bellies and when they're born the hair falls out, as is the case with dolphins. Other animals, like some whales, have completely bare skin and only a few hairs on their heads. Or it could be that the fur had transformed into spines that protect the animal from predators—like hedgehogs, porcupines, and echidnas **(1)**—or hard plates, like pangolins **(2)**.

There are also mammals with so much fur that even the palms of their hands and feet are covered. This is the case with polar bears , which have to stay warm in very cold climates.

There are some mammals that don't like to always wear the same "clothes," such as the Arctic hare **(4)**, which has a brown summer coat and a winter coat that's white as snow! This way, it's always well disguised, whatever the season.

Can mammals be carnivores *and* herbivores?

Of course. Being defined as a mammal is related to what the animal eats right after it's born—its mother's milk. Later, when the animals grow, the different species have very different diets: some eat insects (and are called insectivores), some eat plants (and are called herbivores), and others eat a bit of everything (and are called omnivores, like us).

"Would you like a bite?" ask the carnivores

When we think of carnivores, we may think of big animals like lions, tigers, or killer whales. But there are also much smaller mammals that are brave predators, for example, weasels, which are able to catch rabbits, animals much bigger than they are.

Very cunning omnivores

Some primates, such as chimpanzees, eat animals and vegetables, and because they're so intelligent, they're able to use simple tools to help them feed themselves. For example, if they want to eat fruit that has a hard shell, they use a stone to break it; if they want to eat ants, they use a stick that they push into the anthill to make the ants scurry out. After that, all they have to do is enjoy the snacks!

- -

Did you know that the Etruscan shrew (*Suncus etruscus*) is one of the smallest mammals in the world? It's just 2 in (5 cm) long, and is a greedy predator!

Are there wolves out there?

Well, it depends where you live . . . But don't worry, even if there are wolves in your region, they aren't going to appear in front of you in a city! Wolves always hide away in the most isolated places and don't like getting close to us.

Across the world there are two species of wolf: the gray wolf and the red wolf. The gray wolf once lived almost everywhere on the planet, and was the most widely distributed mammal (except humans, of course!). It's now extinct in lots of European countries, Mexico, and most of the USA, due to being hunted by humans. It was worse with the red wolf, and this species became extinct in the wild in 1980. Luckily, there were still red wolves in captivity and it was possible to reintroduce this species in North Carolina (USA), one of the places where it originally existed.

Do wolves talk, too?

Apart from the big bad wolf in the story of Little Red Riding Hood, no wolf can speak . . . but, even so, wolves communicate very well with one another, not only by howling (when they howl they can be heard, even at a distance, by other wolves) but also through scent and vision. Marks of excrement and urine and also "scratches" (holes made using their claws) are made for other wolves to see and smell.

Do you know what a pack is?

- - - - - - - - -

It's a family of wolves, normally made up of a father, mother, and youngest offspring (and sometimes the older ones, too).

Once a year, in April or May, each she-wolf has about 5 cubs per litter. When these offspring are 1 or 2 years old, they leave their parents and form another family.

What color is the gray wolf?

- - - - - - - - - - - -

This isn't a trick question! The gray wolf can be white with gray, brown, black, cream, or tawny colors and sometimes almost entirely white or black. But, as you can tell from the name, gray is the most common color.

And what about biologists, do they howl, too?

Yes! Biologists who study wolves howl to see if a wolf responds. Because wolves don't like unknown wolves being in their territory, they'll answer any howl just to say: "I'm in charge here, go and howl somewhere else!" So biologists can tell that there are wolves in that area. A good trick, isn't it?

Do you want to know a story about bears?

Everyone knows that bears like honey. In the past, lots of people had beehives to provide them with honey. So, as soon as bears smelled the honey, all they thought about was "attacking" these hives!

This is why, when there were lots of bears in Europe, people built huge walls over 10 ft (3 m) high around beehives. That way the bears couldn't go on their greedy attacks.

Today, there aren't bears in many of these countries, but there are still a lot of traces of their paths in some place names, for example: Bear Hole, Bear Creek, Bear Wood, Bear Valley. Even though they're extinct in many countries in Europe, North Africa, and Asia, brown bears are still common in many Eurasian countries and in North America. There are also seven other species of bear, with the giant panda being the most endangered of all.

Write a book of animal stories

After having read this chapter (and all the other ones about animals) you might have come up with a lot of ideas for stories inspired by the lives of animals. Write and illustrate your ideas.

Draw different mammals

Of course it's not easy to find mammals in nature that will stay still long enough for you to draw them. So, find images and try to draw different animals in this group, looking carefully at their different shapes, legs, mouths and coverings. Drawing is also a way to better understand the things around us.

GLOSSARY

Adaptation
The way an organism becomes more suited to its environment.

Aerodynamic
The properties or qualities of an object in terms of how easily it is able to move through the air.

Amphibian
A member of a group of cold-blooded vertebrate animals.

Annelid
A member of a group of animals comprising segmented worms, including earthworms, lugworms, ragworms, and leeches.

Antenna
A pair of long, sensitive organs.

Anura
A group of amphibians that do not have tails and whose back legs are bigger than their front legs.

Apoda
A group of amphibians that do not have tails or legs and resemble worms.

Articulated antennae
Antennae that are made up of several pieces that are joined together.

Asymmetry
A lack of symmetry—a lack of equality between parts.

Autotomy
The ability of an animal to voluntarily cast off a body part, and still live.

Biodiversity
The variety and abundance of living organisms that exist in a region.

Biologist
A scientist who focuses on the study of living organisms.

Bipedal
An animal that uses two legs for walking.

Blowhole
The respiratory orifice of some marine mammals, which is also used to make sounds.

Botany
The branch of biology that studies plants.

Breed
Mating to produce offspring.

Carnivore
An animal that eats other animals.

Cell
The basic structure of living organisms. Animals and plants, for example, are made up of many millions of cells. Cells are so small that they can only be seen with the help of a microscope.

Chrysalis
The protective case of a caterpillar as it transforms into a butterfly or moth.

Classification
The arrangement of animals into groups according to their similarities and relationships with one another.

Contort
To twist or bend out of shape.

Contract
To reduce in size—the opposite of expanding.

Copulation
Mating to produce offspring.

Core
The central part of an object, such as the tough, center of a fruit, which contains the seeds.

Crustacean
An animal that usually lives in water and has a hard shell, with several pairs of legs.

Dermis
The deepest layer of skin.

Digestion
The process of breaking down food into matter that can either be absorbed by the body or excreted as waste.

Down
The soft, fluffy feathers of a young bird or the insulating layer of feathers underneath a mature bird's other feathers.

Eardrum
A membrane in the ear, which is responsible for the amplification and transmission of sound to the inner ear. Eardrums are frequently visible on amphibians.

Echolocation
The method bats use to detect obstacles, using their hearing. Bats emit sounds that move through space as a wave; when these

sounds "hit" an object, they bounce back to the bat's ears. Then their ears pass the information to the brain, which is able to decipher the surrounding environment.

Ecology

The branch of biology that studies the relationships between organisms and the environment that surrounds them.

Ecosystem

The sum of all the organisms that live in a region, the environment that surrounds them, and all their relationships.

Ectothermic

Animals that regulate their temperature through exchanges of heat with the outside world. They are also called cold-blooded animals. Lizards are an example of this. See also 'endothermic'.

Endangered

A species which is at serious risk of extinction.

Endemic species

A species that only exists in a given region and does not spontaneously occur anywhere else.

Endothermic

Animals capable of regulating their temperature through the production of heat inside the body. Humans, as well as all other mammals, are endothermic.

Entomology

The branch of zoology that studies insects.

Epidermis

The outermost layer of the skin.

Estivation

The state of inactivity of some animals during the summer.

Evolution

Changes in the hereditary characteristics of a species that can occur from one generation to another. This process means that species change and diversify over time, adapting to the changing environment and giving rise to others.

Excrement

Feces, or what we might commonly call poop.

Exoskeleton

The external skeleton of certain animals, made of chitin.

Exotic species

A species introduced in a place to which it is not native.

Extinction

The disappearance of a species. We say that a species is extinct when all the organisms in that species have died.

Exuvia

The cast-off exoskeleton of an animal.

Feces

Another word for the excrement (or waste

matter) that is left behind after food has been digested.

Fertilization
The union of male and female reproductive cells, giving rise to an ovum, the beginning of a new living being.

Fossil
The name given to the remains of plants or animals that are found in layers of the Earth from thousands or millions of years ago.

Frugivore
An animal that eats fruit. (Therefore, a fructivore is also a herbivore.)

Fungi
A group of simple organisms which eat decaying material or other living things.

Gelatinous
Something which is gel-like in texture.

Genus
A category of animals or plants within the same family, which have been grouped together due to them sharing common characteristics.

Geology
The science that studies the Earth (the composition of rocks, the evolution of our planet, earthquakes, etc.).

Gland
An organ that produces chemical substances with specific functions in organisms (hormones, for example).

Global warming
The gradual increase in a planet's temperature due to the trapping of the sun's heat in its atmosphere.

GPS
An abbreviation of *global positioning system*. This is a system that allows us to find our exact location using information sent to artificial satellites orbiting the Earth.

Greenhouse gas
Gases which are responsible for global warming.

Granivore
An animal which mostly eats seeds and grain.

Gynoecium
A flower's carpels, its female reproductive organs. The carpels are formed of stigma, styles, and ovaries and can be free or joined together. The term *pistil* is commonly used to describe a free carpel or several carpels joined together. A flower can have one or many pistils.

Gypsobelum
A kind of "dart" produced by some species of gastropod (snails, slugs, etc.) that is part of their reproductive apparatus. Before copulation, the gypsobelum is introduced into the mate to make it more receptive.

This is also called a dart or love dart.

Habitat
A location with the conditions necessary for the survival of a species.

Herbivore
An animal that eats plants.

Hermaphrodite
An organism that has both male and female reproductive organs.

Herpetology
The branch of zoology that studies reptiles and amphibians.

Hibernation
The state of inactivity of some animals during winter that allows them to save energy. Some species bury themselves or hide in caves and stay there to sleep for several weeks or months.

Hormones
Chemical substances produced by organisms that circulate inside them (almost always in the blood). One of their functions is to allow organisms to communicate with one another.

Ichthyology
The branch of zoology that studies fish.

Infinite
A measurement that is endless.

Insectivore
An animal that eats insects. (An insectivore can be considered a special kind of carnivore.)

Invertebrate
An animal that lacks a backbone or spinal column.

Jurassic
A period in the history of our planet that happened millions of years ago (but precisely between 199.6 and 145.5 million years ago).

Larva
The state of some animals before they become adults. Larvae do not reproduce. They can look like adults (as is the case with cockroaches), or they can look very different (as is the case with butterflies).

Lateral
Something which relates to the side of an object.

Lobulated
Something which has lobes, or is divided into lobes (a round shape, such as the shape of an earlobe).

Luminous
Something which gives off light.

Malacology
The branch of zoology that studies mollusks.

Mammal
A member of a group of vertebrate animals which grow hair or fur and are warm-blooded, who also produce milk to feed their young.

Mammalogy
The branch of zoology that studies mammals.

Marsupial
A member of a group of mammals which are not born fully developed but continue to grow in a pouch on their mother's belly.

Marsupium
The name of the pouch on the belly of a marsupial, which is used to carry their young.

Metamorphosis
A drastic alteration in form that some animals go through (butterflies, for example) when they change from larva to adult.

Migration
The seasonal movement of animals from one area to another.

Mmicry
The ability of animals to change their appearance to match the environment around them and therefore go unnoticed. Chameleons have this ability.

Mollusk
A member of a group of invertebrate animals which have soft bodies and are usually covered in a shell.

Native species
A species that exists in a region and was not taken there artificially (i.e., by humans).

Nectar
A sugary liquid produced by flowers that is used to attract pollinators.

Nocturnal
Being active during the night.

Nuptial flight
The flight of some insects, during which adults mate with one another.

Nymph
One of the stages of insect metamorphosis, between larva and adult.

Omnivore
An animal that eats both plants and animals.

Orifice

An opening in an object or body.

Ornithology

The branch of zoology that studies birds.

Ornithologist

Oviparous

An animal whose offspring develop in eggs, outside the mother. Birds are the most common example.

Ovoviviparous

An animal whose offspring develop inside eggs, inside the mother's body. In other words, the eggs are laid when the offspring are ready to be born.

Ovule

A female reproductive cell.

Parotid glands

These are glands in amphibians that produce a milky substance used as defense against predators.

Parthenogenesis

The process by which a female produces an embryo without fertilization taking place.

Pellet

Undigested remains regurgitated by animals; pellets are often used by biologists to study the diet of certain species.

Permeable

Allowing liquid or gas to pass through it. The opposite of permeable is impermeable.

Pheromones

Chemical substances that organisms produce and that spread out through the air (or water) to "communicate" with other organisms of the same species.

Pineal eye

An organ that exists on the top of the head of some reptiles (and certain other animals). It is not used to see, but only to give an idea of the light around the animal.

Piscivore

An animal that eats fish. (A piscivore can be considered a special kind of carnivore.)

Pollen

Minute grains produced by the male organs of flowers (stamen) that carry the male reproductive cells. When these cells join with female reproductive cells (ovules), they give rise to seeds.

Pollination

The sexual act of plants, or the passage of pollen from stamen to the gynoecium. When this happens within a flower or between two flowers on the same plant, it is called self-pollination; when it happens between flowers on different plants, it is called cross-pollination.

Pollinators

Elements that help plants carry out

pollination. They may be various kinds of animals such as insects, birds, or mammals, or agents that are not living things, such as the wind (anemophily) or water (hydrophily), or humans (artificial).

Polychaete
A group of marine worms which share certain characteristics.

Predator
An animal that kills another animal in order to eat it.

Prey
An animal killed by another organism for food.

Proboscis
A long appendage protruding from the head of an animal, such as the mouth of a butterfly or the trunk of an elephant.

Pupa
An insect during the stage when it transforms from larva into an adult.

Rachis
A hard, central shaft—such as the shaft of a feather or stem of a plant.

Radula
A band of tiny teeth in mollusks, which break up food so that it can be swallowed.

Regeneration
The act of forming or being created again.

Regurgitation
The act of returning incompletely digested food from the stomach to the mouth.

Reproduction
The way living things produce other living things, their descendants, which continue the species. Reproduction can be sexual, when sex cells from two living things (female and male) come together, or asexual, when a single living thing produces another one exactly like it (as in parthenogenesis or when plants grow roots that produce other plants).

Reptile
A member of a group of cold-blooded, vertebrate animals which lay eggs on land and have skin covered with bony plates (or scales).

Retractable
Something which can be drawn back in, such as a claw.

Sap
A liquid formed of sugars and other nutrients, almost always produced by the leaves of plants.

Scientific name
All species of living things have a scientific name. This is formed of two parts: the first is the genus and must be written with a capital letter; the second is called the species. Both should be written in italics.

Segment

A part of something. To be segmented is to be divided up into parts.

Seta

Stiff, hair-like structures.

Species

A group of organisms that is able to reproduce together and have fertile offspring.

Spermatozoid

A male reproductive cell. When it joins with an ovule, they make a fertilized egg, which then develops into an embryo.

Spur

A sharp, pointed object.

Stamen

The male reproductive organs of a flower where pollen is stored.

Symmetry

Balanced proportions—the quality of having equality between parts.

Tadpole

The form of amphibians when they are young (larvae).

Toxins

Poisonous substances produced by living organisms to defend themselves from predators.

Transparent

Allowing light to pass through it. If something is transparent, it is possible to see through it to objects behind it.

Tundra

A large, flat Arctic region of Europe, North America and Asia where the land is permanently frozen.

Undulated

A wavy surface or edge.

Urodela

A group of amphibians that have tails and whose back legs and front legs are roughly the same length.

Vertebrate

An animal with a backbone or spinal column.

Vermicomposting

The process of worms turning organic waste (like food waste) into fertilizer for the soil.

Viscera

Another word for an animal's internal organs.

Viviparous

An animal whose offspring develop inside the mother's body. Mammals are viviparous. (Us humans are, too, because we're mammals.)

Vocal sacs

Skin membranes that many amphibians have in their throats or the sides of their mouths that serve to amplify sound when they want to call a mate or give warnings.

Voracious

Being eager to eat a large quantity of food.

Vulnerable species

A species at risk of extinction. This is one of the eight categories of threat used to classify species. The others are: *Extinct, Extinct in the Wild, Critically Endangered, Endangered, Near Threatened, Least Concern*. This classification is used internationally and is represented in the IUCN (International Union for the Conservation of Nature) Red List.

Zoology

The branch of biology that studies animals.

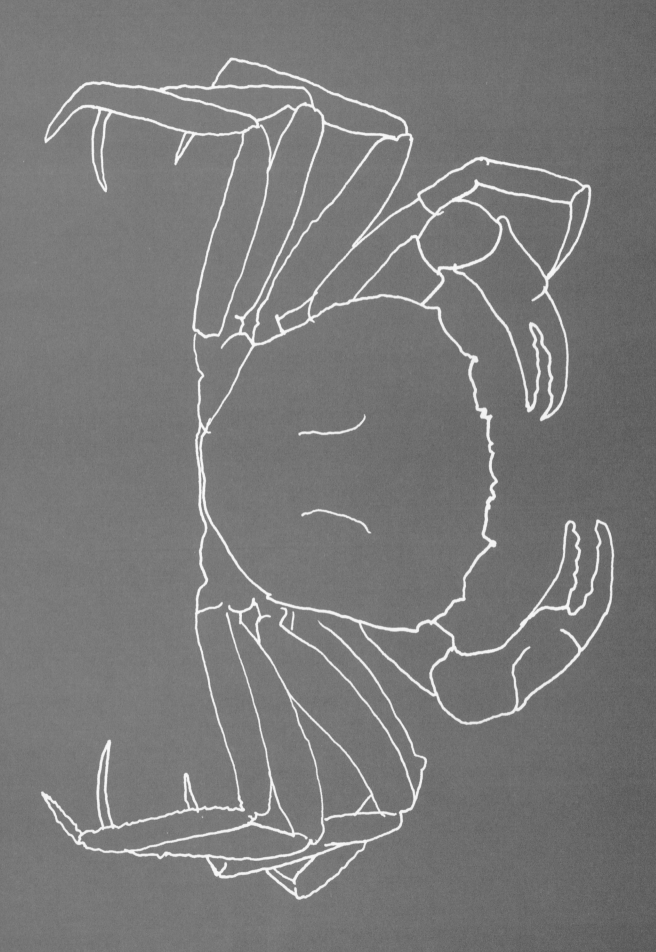

TIMELINE
IMPORTANT DATES

350 BC (approx.)

The Greek philosopher Aristotle collects examples of fauna and flora to group them according to their characteristics. This is the first classification of living things that we know of.

1632

Birth of Benedict de Spinoza, the philosopher who understood nature as a continuation of God. For Spinoza, stones, animals, and plants all have a body and mind.

1735

The botanist Carl von Linné (known as Linnaeus) publishes the first edition of *Systema Naturae*—the system of classification used, even today, to classify living things according to what we call their scientific name.

1866

Ernst Haeckel first coins the term "ecology" to describe the study of the relationship between organisms and where they live. The word comes from the Greek "logos" (study) and "oikos" (home).

1872

In the United States, a bill is passed by Congress and signed into law by President Grant to create the world's first national park. Yellowstone National Park now comprises more than 2 million acres.

1895

The National Trust is founded in the UK to preserve outdoor spaces and prevent them from being built on. Today they are the UK's biggest land owner.

1915

In the UK, banker and expert naturalist Charles Rothschild holds a meeting to discuss his radical idea about saving places for nature. This meeting leads to the creation of the Society for the Promotion of Nature Reserves (SPNR) and signals the beginning of UK nature conservation.

1915

The Ecological Society of America, a nonprofit organization of scientists, is formed. Within two years, the ESA has 307 members.

1949

The book *A Sand County Almanac*, by Aldo Leopold, considered the father of wild ecology, is published. One of his most famous quotes is that we must learn to "think like a mountain."

1960

The British scientist James Lovelock proposes a theory known as the Gaia hypothesis, in which he presents the Earth as a unique living organism that is able to regulate itself in many ways.

1962

The biologist Rachel Carson publishes the book *Silent Spring*, in which she shows the risks of unregulated use of pesticides (DDT), especially to birds. This book led to a revolution in environmental laws.

1970

Earth Day is celebrated for the first time, on the April 22, in the United States.

1970

The European Council launches the European Year of Nature Conservation.

1971

Two of the world's most important environmental association are created: Friends of the Earth International and Greenpeace.

1973

Arne Naess introduces the concept of "deep ecology." For this Norwegian philosopher and mountaineer, nature is not just something to be manipulated for our benefit; it is a place for us to share, equally.

1973

The Convention on International Trade in Endangered Species of Wild Fauna and Flora (CITES) is approved, prohibiting the sale and purchase of thousands of endangered species.

1987

Introduction of the concept of "sustainable development," which demonstrates that the economy, people, and the environment must be linked, bearing the needs of future generations in mind.

1992

In Rio de Janeiro, world leaders meet to discuss the planet's environmental situation (at a conference known as ECO 92).

1997

Year of the Kyoto Protocol, which lays out goals for the reduction of global greenhouse gases, which are responsible for global warming.

2007/2009

The General Assembly of the United Nations dedicated the period between 2007 and 2009 for commemorations of International Year of Planet Earth.

2010

The United Nations declares 2010 International Year of Biodiversity.

If you want to know more . . .

Here are some organizations that work in the area of nature conservation or study. Check the websites to learn more about their activities:

Worldwide:

BirdLife International
- www.birdlife.org

Conservation International
Environmental organisation
- www.conservation.org

Earth Island Institute
- www.earthisland.org

Earthwatch Institute
- earthwatch.org

International Union for Conservation of Nature
- www.iucn.org

Oceana
- na.oceana.org

The Nature Conservancy
- www.nature.org

UNEP-WCMC United Nations Environment Programme
- www.unep-wcmc.org

UNESCO United Nations Educational, Scientific and Cultural Organization
- en.unesco.org

WCS Wildlife Conservation Society
- www.wcs.org

WWF World Wide Fund for Nature
- www.worldwildlife.org

In the US:

AMNH American Museum of Natural History
- www.amnh.org

National Audubon Society
- www.audubon.org

NPCA National Park Conservation Association
- www.npca.org

NPS National Park Service
- www.nps.gov

SCA Student Conservation Association
- www.thesca.org

In Australia and New Zealand:

ACF Australian Conservation Foundation
- www.acfonline.org.au

Government of South Australia Department of Environment, Water and Natural Resources
- www.environment.sa.gov.au

NZ Department of Conservation
- www.doc.govt.nz

Parks Australia
- www.parksaustralia.gov.au

In the UK:

Friends of the Earth
- www.foe.co.uk

Greenpeace
- www.greenpeace.org.uk

JNCC Joint Nature Conservation Committee
- www.jncc.defra.gov.uk

The National Trust
- www.nationaltrust.org.uk

RSPB Royal Society for the Protection of Birds
- www.rspb.org.uk

The Wildlife Trusts
- www.wildlifetrusts.org